# Our Debt to Greece and Rome

EDITORS
GEORGE DEPUE HADZSITS, PH.D.

DAVID MOORE ROBINSON, PH.D., LL.D.

# PLAUTUS AND TERENCE

BY      *1880 –*

## GILBERT NORWOOD, M.A.

COOPER  SQUARE  PUBLISHERS,  INC.

NEW YORK

1963

Published 1963 by Cooper Square Publishers, Inc.
59 Fourth Avenue, New York 3, N. Y.
Library of Congress Catalog Card No. 63-10276

PRINTED IN THE UNITED STATES OF AMERICA

# PREFACE

THROUGHOUT this book I have adhered to my intention of discussing Plautus and Terence as dramatists. That is my justification for offering conclusions less traditional than is customary in such brief treatises; anyone who discusses these plays as plays will find that the present condition of Terentian and, still more, of Plautine scholarship compels him to write controversially if he loves good work and hates bad.

That the *Mercator* should be read by only one student for every hundred who read the *Captivi* is a fantastic perversion rendered possible only by a complete indifference to the very nature of drama. The depreciation of Terence is mainly due to the same cause. For many years scholars were content to study these works as documents of early Latin, as a mine of " allusions," as exercises in metre and rhythm, as anything rather than what their authors intended. Now that drama in English-speaking lands has become once more a living art, it is high time that Latin plays should be appreciated and (when possible) enjoyed as plays, not as bits of mummy.

Two acknowledgments should be made. Mr. Basil Blackwell of Oxford has most kindly allowed me to draw on my book, *The Art of Terence*, published by him in 1923. I take this, the first, opportunity to offer the American Council of Learned Societies my warmest thanks for a grant that enabled me to make a tour, no less illuminating than delightful, in Greece during the spring of this year.

GILBERT NORWOOD

*Toronto, December 9, 1931*

# CONTENTS

# CONTENTS

# PLAUTUS AND TERENCE

# PLAUTUS AND TERENCE

## I. INTRODUCTION

A GRAVE error lies in wait for us at the very threshold: to imagine that the phrase "Plautus and Terence" indicates some kind of partnership, or that these poets were (so to put it) elder and younger brother. Plautus, it is implied, was indeed, strong and boisterous, Terence, weak and elegant; but both "wrote comedies," both borrowed from Greece the social drama of young lover and distressed maid, the villainous slave-dealer and the cunning valet, the shameless parasite and the stupid old father. This assertion, though it contains fact, is gravely misleading. The work of Terence is high comedy, that of Plautus mostly farce.[1]

A second mistake is that these playwrights, however they differ in technique and temperament, are comparable on their merits. The overwhelming majority of critics have maintained that, while Terence is reasonably good, Plautus is distinctly better. The present writer regards this view as a grave mistake. We must here anticipate what will be discussed later, and remark that although a small portion of Plautus' surviving work (perhaps one-seventh) is, for reasons that have little to do with his own talents, distinctly good, even brilliant, Plautus is in the remainder of his writing, despite a few good patches, on the whole and in regard to the most fundamental aspects of a playwright's work, the worst of all writers who have ever won permanent repute. The details must be for the moment postponed. Here it will suffice to say that the full horror of his ineptitude lies not in crudity of ideas, language, or construction, frequent as this is. No: the offence that puts Plautus outside the pale of art, almost of civilization, is his practice of tying together — not only in the same play, sometimes in the same scene — modes of feeling and treatment utterly incongruous. For example: a dramatist whose play assumes that sexual irregularity is normal and amusing must preserve that atmosphere at all costs. If he remarks at intervals: " Hm! Ladies and Gentlemen, I know that all this is — hm! — very, very wrong," he becomes merely nauseating. This Plautus has achieved.[2] In *Amphitruo* he

[ 4 ]

does far worse, so much worse that one simply
cannot discuss the play freely. It shows how
the king of the gods made Alcmena the mother
of Hercules, despite her wisdom and chastity,
because he used his power of miracles to as-
sume the likeness of her husband. It may be
answered: " Do not judge an ancient poet by
modern standards based on an utterly different
theology." But the objection lies not against
lower theology or unenlightened ethics. The
point is that Plautus destroys his own position:
for example, we are to adore Jupiter and we
are to see him as a lecherous swindler. Methods may be imagined of rendering the story,
if it must be rendered, without too much offence; but a blend of horseplay, wifely dignity,
lewd jests, and celestial splendour is not among
them. Corresponding sins of dramatic technique are frequent. Terence, on the other
hand, we shall find reason to consider not
merely a most excellent writer, but a writer on
an utterly different level — except for that
strange one-seventh of Plautus.

But before we proceed to discuss these
twenty-six dramas, decency suggests that we
should face one question: " If Plautus is so
bad, why has everyone been mistaken about

him? " *Securus iudicat orbis terrarum:* there
is no appeal against a universal verdict.  What
excuse can we find for such hardihood?  There
are at least four reasons, applicable in different
ages.

The Roman world, though the merits of
Plautus were impugned or belittled by two
distinguished writers, Horace [3] and Quintilian,[4]
certainly rated him highly.  But the Romans
never had any genuine feeling for the drama.
Tragedy, comedy and farce all dwindled away
after a brief activity in Republican days; later,
Seneca was a mere rhetorician, not a man of
the theatre at all; the mimes,[5] which were indeed popular throughout antiquity and the Byzantine Age, possessed (so far as we can learn)
no genuinely dramatic quality.  Cultivated
Romans preferred rhetoric in various forms,
uncultivated Romans preferred gladiators or
vaudeville entertainers.  The praises we hear
of Plautus are remarks made by literary readers who admired his Latin and his jokes, not
his dramaturgy.[6]

In the modern world we may detect three
causes.  First, our main impression about the
Romans being that they spent their days in sur-
rounding the enemy, espousing the causes of

their clients in the law-courts, and (more generally) in giving off *gravitas,* we are so delighted and amazed by the discovery of a Roman who makes jokes and depicts love-affairs that we fall into a stupor of admiration utterly impervious to the badness of the jokes and the pettiness of the intrigue. The emptiest cinema-story ever exhibited has a Sophoclean subtlety if compared with the *Asinaria;* but people who would not dream of enduring a modern work that even approached this level, beam delightedly whenever Plautus is mentioned, simply because, in an age otherwise unfamiliar to us, he writes of things familiar to us indeed. "Fancy a man in a toga talking about bacon! How thrillingly laughable! " Next, those who have expounded Latin literature have too often known deplorably little about drama in general. One writer on Plautus offers these astounding remarks: " Mr. Gillette is credited with having written in *Secret Service* the first aside-less play. But this is abnormal and rather an affectation of technical skill. The aside is an accepted convention." This in 1918! The achievements of Ibsen, and the revolution wrought by them in the drama of Europe and America, had still not reached his ears.

Thirdly, during the last generation we have had to count with the attacks on classical studies and the consequent propagandism of their defenders. That defence has been vigorous, learned and skilful, but not entirely sagacious. In our natural ardour to preserve the study of Homer and Plato, Virgil and Tacitus, we have reared a fortification round all the writers of ancient Europe and have implied that they all equally merit our perishing upon the rampart in their defence. The results of this indiscriminate fervour are at times quaint. *Plutus* is edited and read as often as *Hippolytus;* grave eulogies of Caesar's "style" are printed; Cicero's most vapid journalism is extolled beside his *Pro Cluentio;* and Plautus is placed at least as high as Terence, whereas Terence surpasses all writers of high comedy except Menander and Molière, while Plautus occupies the exact nadir of dramatic art.

The third and last misconception that we have to dispel is concerned with the originality of the two poets. There is no doubt, there never has been doubt, that they both derive much from Greek New Comedy, now surviving only in fragments [7] great or small. But what

[ 8 ]

are we to make of this undoubted fact? There
are certain lines of study that we are justified
in following. We may endeavour to detect in
the Latin plays: elements entirely borrowed
from Greek — more or less close translations;
elements entirely original with Plautus or Terence — matter that had no original or even
analogue in the Greek; and the obvious re-
siduum — elements inspired by the Greek but
freely reshaped. Again, we may attempt, using
the results just described and any other evidence, to reconstruct the lost Greek comedies.
And, again using those results, we may describe
the originality of the Roman playwrights: its
limits, the features of dramatic art in which it
is more evident or less, and the light all this
throws upon the mind and character of Plautus
or of Terence, upon Roman culture and upon
matters of even wider scope. But we are *not*
justified in altering our opinion of the Latin
plays themselves. One too often sees the implication that the plays of Terence deserve less
admiration because of his debt to Greece, and
that the faults of Plautus do not exist if they
can be attributed to his originals. The thing
has come to such a pass that we need to state
plainly a rather absurd doctrine: if a Teren-

tian play is good, a Plautine play bad, then good and bad they are. The origin of certain features can make no difference whatever to these verdicts.

It nevertheless remains to be said that, quite apart from literary and dramatic excellence or demerit, much interest resides for us in these works. They provide the student of language with a great mass of early Latin, the metrist with abundant material for the study of metre and rhythm, the historian of literature with information about the plots of lost Greek comedies and with the originals of many modern plays or parts of plays. Above all, the student of social history will fasten eagerly upon these twenty-six dramas: this is what Romans heard, watched and enjoyed in the age of the Punic Wars. Terence, it is true, pleased only the small minority who studied Greek, such men as the Scipionic circle in his own day, Cicero in a later age. But who can read the prologue of the *Eunuchus* without a thrill? Here is a genuine personal document from Rome in the second century before Christ, echoing the discussions and rivalries of literary cliques, a little back-door suddenly opened on life as it was then lived, taking us directly into

the house — unlike the histories and procla-
mations that reveal rather the countryside sur-
rounding the mansion, and the Roman eagle
beating his way from horizon to horizon. In
this sense Plautus is invaluable. For an hour
we may sit beside the stolid heroes who bore
arms in the greatest war of antiquity. The
outcries of Euclio, the bogus ghost-story of the
*Mostellaria*, Pseudolus' machinations, and that
piteous duet of the shipwrecked maidens, fell
upon the ears of veterans who, after fifteen
terrific years, had beaten Hannibal out of
Italy. Here is a voice from the still-living
past: Plautus worked many years before the
Gracchi started the Roman people down that
long road leading to Augustus, Diocletian and
Constantine.

These introductory discussions are intended,
not only to indicate the best frame of mind in
which to approach these two writers, but also
to account for the bifurcation of treatment that
is to follow. After a brief statement of one
common feature, we shall speak of Plautus and
Terence separately. They both treat as a rule
the same theme. Their methods of handling
it differ immensely, but their starting-point in
most of the twenty-six comedies varies only in

detail. Let us give a "composite photograph" of the stories in these works.

A young Athenian is in love with a charming but friendless girl who is the purchased slave of a *leno,* or professional procurer. This man is either already hiring her out to anyone who will pay, or is on the point of selling her to some unpleasant person, usually a military officer (the famous *miles*). The hero is at his wits' end. He wishes to purchase her and keep her as his mistress: he cannot legally marry her, as she is not of Athenian birth. But he has not the sum demanded by the girl's owner; how, then, is he to rescue her? Here intervenes his slave, loyal to his young master but otherwise conscienceless, who saves the situation by an elaborate ruse either to defraud the hero's father of the needed sum or to induce the slave-owner to part with the girl. When discovery of this deception arrives, all is put right by a sudden revelation that the heroine is really of Athenian birth (but kidnapped or lost in babyhood) and can therefore marry the hero.

These persons, young man and girl, slave-owner, bullying stupid soldier, cunning valet, and curmudgeonly father were stock charac-

ters. The parasite — an insinuating greedy
hanger-on — the honest slave and the hero's
friend were also frequent. That this scheme,
as a scheme, is derived from Greek Comedy,
there can be no doubt. Our poets, in their
prologues, themselves tell us often that "this
play is the So-and-So of Diphilus" or Menander or Philemon. Donatus,[8] the invaluable
commentator on Terence, indicates as much;
but there is no need to enumerate all the witnesses. We must, however, beware of trading
unduly on such correspondence: it is, for instance, beyond controversy that considerable
passages in Plautus are entirely his own. Two
dramas may have the same "story" but may
diverge so much in the handling thereof that
only by an effort do we realize the similarity
in their foundations. In this sense Aeschylus'
*Choephoroe* and Shakespeare's *Hamlet* are the
same.

Details of the conditions under which these
plays were presented — theatre-buildings, cos-
tumes, methods of performance, the festivals
and the officials concerned, and so forth —
need not be fully set out now, as they have
been excellently described elsewhere.[9] All
plays were performed in an open-air theatre.

[ 13 ]

The stage usually represented a street along which stood houses where the chief characters lived in convenient proximity. Interiors were never shown: all the action passed in front of the houses, however unnatural that may seem. Even the heroine at her dressing-table in the *Mostellaria* is placed outside, but no doubt this scene, like drinking-parties, was enacted in a portico. The most private conversations were carried on in the street. Dramatic structure might thus become absurdly simple: if a plot was being hatched, another person could sidle up, explaining to the audience " I will listen to what they are saying," and gain information enough to thwart his opponents. Soliloquies and asides were common. The plays are divided into acts,[10] but these divisions are usually of no importance, since there is rarely any considerable lapse of time to be imagined, the place of the action remains unchanged, and there were no choric performances between the acts as in fifth-century Athens. Nevertheless, purely incidental music was sometimes given during these intervals.[11]

# II. PLAUTUS: GENERAL REMARKS

TITUS MACCUS [12] PLAUTUS was born about 254 B.C. at Sarsina in Umbria, a region of north central Italy. This town was near the border of Cisalpine Gaul and had been conquered by Rome only twelve years before Plautus' birth. Probably therefore his native speech was Umbrian, not Latin: his splendid mastery of the latter was no doubt acquired in Rome itself, to which city he removed at an early age. There for some years he earned his livelihood by theatrical work, of a kind which we cannot specify with confidence. The name Maccus strongly suggests that he was an actor, since this was the name borne by one of the stock characters in Atellane farces. But our authorities [13] report that he worked *in operis artificum scenicorum*, which implies manual work, such as scene-shifting or stage-carpentry. He saved money, which he invested in trade and lost. Apparently he himself travelled on this venture, for we read that he returned to Rome in poverty. Perhaps it was during this period that he acquired his complete knowledge of Greek. Next he became the servant of a baker who employed him to work the mill; but he found time and energy to begin dramatic composition, and to this period three of his lost plays belong. Meeting with success, he became free to devote himself to literature, which he did until his death. It is not known whether he became a Roman citizen. One hundred and thirty plays were attributed to him, but the learned Varro [14] recognized as genuine only twenty-one — the twenty that we now possess and the *Vidularia,* whereof only fragments survive. A few of our comedies can be dated. The *Miles* was probably written before 205, since it mentions (211 f.) the imprisonment of Naevius, which ended in 206, as a present fact; *Stichus* is dated at 200 by its *didascalia* (the official details, including the consuls of the year, prefixed to the text); the *Trinummus* cannot be earlier than 194, for it mentions (990) "the new aediles"; the *Aulularia* must be later than 195, for it assumes (498 ff.) the abrogation of the Oppian Law, which occurred in that year; *Pseudolus* is dated by its *didascalia* at 191; *Bacchides* belongs probably to 189, since it refers (1072 ff.) to

[ 16 ]

the four triumphs of that year; *Epidicus* is earlier than *Bacchides*, which alludes to it by name (214). Plautus died in 184.[15]

An ancient epitaph [16] runs:

*postquam est mortem aptus Plautus, comoedia luget,*
*scaena est deserta, dein risus ludu' iocusque*
*et numeri innumeri simul omnes conlacrimarunt.*

" Now that Plautus has found death, Comedy mourns, the stage is desolate, laughter, fun, jest and numbers unnumbered all together burst into tears." (The " numbers " are the various rhythms that he employed.) His reputation flourished so effectually that his works were often revived,[17] and probably revised for such occasions, to which some of the existing prologues must be referred. Thus the prologue of the *Casina* looks back to the Plautine era with humble admiration:

*ea tempestate flos poetarum fuit,*
*qui nunc abierunt hinc in communem locum.*

" In that age was the flower of poets, who have now gone hence to the place that awaits all." Plautus' repute, though he appears to have been almost unknown in the Middle Ages, stood high in antiquity. An older contemporary of Cicero, one Volcacius Sedigitus,[18] in his "canon" of the comic playwrights puts Plautus second (after Caecilius), and Terence only sixth. The versatile Aelius Stilo exclaimed that if the Muses had wished to speak Latin they would have used the style of Plautus.[19] His famous pupil Varro held that whereas Caecilius "demands the palm" for plot, and Terence for characterization, Plautus demands it for his dialogue (*sermones*).[20] Cicero ranks him with the Athenian poets for his "elegant, polished, ingenious and witty manner of jesting," [21] and even puts into the mouth of the orator Crassus a statement that his mother-in-law's speech reminded him of Plautus' style.[22] In the lady's interests, if for no other reason, we may imagine that Cicero was less familiar with our poet than he implies. Centuries later Sidonius Apollinaris exclaimed that Plautus surpasses in charm the wits of Greece.[23] These ecstatic judgments are to be explained partly by patriotism, still more by the fact that their authors considered style only. No ancient critics except Horace and Quintilian seem to have thought of judging this dramatist by his dramatic qualities. Even Quintilian's famous remark is but negative:

[ 18 ]

" Comedy is the lame dog of our literature." [24]
But the comment of Horace [25] is definite:

*adspice, Plautus . . .*
*quam non adstricto percurrat pulpita socco.*
*gestit enim nummum in loculos demittere, post hoc*
*securus cadat an recto stet fabula talo.*

" See how slipshod is Plautus as he hurries
across the boards — he is eager to drop the
cash into his purse, and then he cares nothing
whether his play tumbles or stands upright."
We are to see later how entirely this is justified — save as to the poet's greed. The construction of some among his plays is so incredibly bad that even stupidity alone, even
ignorance alone, even indifference alone, seem
insufficient to explain it. We can but suppose
that he neither knew nor cared what a drama
is, and was concerned with nothing save to
amuse an audience that knew and cared not
indeed less, but no more. He took for this
purpose amusing Greek plays and happened to
produce excellent matter when he happened to
put in little of his own. Horace further [26] attacks Plautus where he seems less assailable:

*at vestri proavi Plautinos et numeros et*
*laudavere sales, nimium patienter utrumque,*
*ne dicam stulte, mirati.*

" But your ancestors praised both the rhythms and the wit of Plautus, admiring both too tolerantly, not to say foolishly." Horace is protesting against the taste of his own day, which depreciated Augustan poetry and sentimentally cried up the earliest Latin work. He is generally thought to have been too severe and too uncritical; Leo, for instance, has written an elaborate rebuttal [27] of his charges against Plautus.

His work, like that of Terence, belonged to the class called *palliatae,* from the *pallium,* or Greek dress, since his plays treat of Greek life; comedies dealing with Roman life were called *togatae.* Fifteen of his surviving works handle the subject already described — the love-entanglements of young men: *Asinaria* (" Tale of a Donkey "), *Aulularia* (" Tale of a Pot "), *Bacchides* (" The Bacchis Sisters "), *Cistellaria* (" Tale of a Chest "), *Curculio* (" Weevil " — the parasite's name), *Epidicus* (name of the contriving slave), *Mercator* (" The Merchant "), *Miles Gloriosus* (" The Braggart Soldier "), *Mostellaria* (" Tale of a Ghost "), *Persa* (" The Persian "), *Poenulus* (" The Lad from Carthage "), *Pseudolus* (" Crafty Liar " — name of the contriving slave), *Rudens*

("The Rope"), *Trinummus* ("The Little Coin"), *Truculentus* ("The Boor" — a slave's name). Of the remaining five, *Amphitruo* depicts Jupiter's metamorphosis into the likeness of the Theban king Amphitryon, and its results, as outlined above; the *Captivi* ("Prisoners") which is unique for having no love-interest, shows a master and slave captured in war and the noble loyalty of the slave, who gains his master's liberation at terrible risk; *Casina* (a slave's name) exhibits the attempts of an elderly married man to get a slave-girl into his power by marrying her to a subservient steward. Concerning the *Vidularia* we know little: the name means "A Tale of a Portmanteau"; probably the basic idea resembled that of the *Rudens*. *Amphitruo* the poet himself describes (59 ff.) as tragi-comedy.

It is desirable, before we study Plautus' work directly, to place him in an historical light, for the sole reason that there are elements in his work that we cannot understand otherwise.

Latin literature begins with Lucius Livius Andronicus, a Greek who translated the *Odyssey* and Greek plays, both tragic and comic, into uncouth Latin. The earliest performance of such a Latin play occurred in 240 B.C. His successor, Cn. Naevius, a Campanian, seems to have been the first Latin writer with any genuine claim to literary merit. He translated both tragedies and comedies, and began to stage his work in 235. Three famous writers followed, almost contemporary with one another. Ennius (239–169) is chiefly celebrated for his epic *Annales*, but he also wrote plays. The other two specialized: Pacuvius (220–132) composed tragedies only; Plautus, comedy — as a rough classification. Here then were already two models that Plautus could imitate: the Greek plays themselves and the methods of blent translation and adaptation that had been followed by Andronicus and Naevius. Was Euripides, the Attic tragedian, a third? [28] It is perfectly true that a number of features in the Plautine works are Euripidean, for instance, the complaint (*Mercator* 817 ff.) that infidelity in a husband is allowed but in a wife means ruin. Yet it is almost certain that the idea was not taken directly from Euripides: a very similar passage is found in Menander's *Arbitration*. No doubt Menander took the germ of the idea from Euripides, who assuredly exercised a strong influence upon Greek Middle and New Comedy; it is therefore unsafe to affirm that Plautus anywhere borrows directly from him. Much the same kind of doubt is attached to the mime, an entertainment immensely popular throughout the Greek world, and enormously long-lived: its earliest great practitioner was Sophron [29] of Syracuse in the fifth century B.C., and it flourished till late Byzantine times. The mimes came to Rome from Magna Graecia (the Greek cities of Southern Italy) and grew steadily in favour. But we cannot point to any feature in Plautus' work that was certainly derived from them, for there also existed purely Italian performances not dissimilar.

The Italian compositions available for his imitation were of three kinds: the *Satura*, the Fescennine verses, and the Atellane farces. *Satura*, though it developed into what we understand by satire, was originally a medley of songs and amusing stories, sung and recited to music with dance and pantomime: it was dramatic merely in the sense that it was acted. The *Fescennini* were crude lampoons and (it seems) never really dramatic at all, though their form was dialogue, or rather an interchange of amusing vituperation. Only the

[ 23 ]

*Atellanae* appear to have possessed genuine dramatic quality — they had a plot, however simple, though the dialogue itself was improvised. There was a great deal of gesture here also, and much indecency; the actors wore masks. The characters were fixed and had always the same names — Maccus, Dossennus, etc. These plays appear to have resembled the coarsest type of Greek mime.

Such were the elements that Plautus found available in addition to his own experience of life, contemporary events and social conditions. His important debts are three: to the New Comedy of Greece for the "story" and very often for the verbal matter itself, though the amount of this varies greatly from play to play; to Andronicus and Naevius for the method of translation — close if necessary, but rarely smelling of its origin; to the Atellanes for crude popular clowning and wealth of gesticulation. The frequent *cantica* (or lyrical monodies) were almost certainly not derived from Greek comedies.[30] It has been asserted,[31] on the other side, that Plautus not only wrote *cantica* out of his own head, but actually invented this kind of composition. A passage of the historian Livy [32] shows however that this kind of work was already produced by Livius Andronicus. Its most probable origin is the *Satura*. However that may be, when Plautus took a comedy of Athens and "turned it into barbarian speech"[33] the alterations were often thorough-going. Besides the elaborate and lengthy *cantica*, we find numerous and striking passages that refer to Roman, not Greek, life and conditions. Again, the structure will often show that he has mortised into his version of one comedy a scene or scenes taken from some other: the practice was called *contaminatio*. Finally, his own verbal style is as a rule very different from the pellucid and sophisticated manner of the Greek playwrights.

Plautus' method of combining much of his own with matter directly translated has not only deeply affected his dramaturgy, but has left strange marks upon the manner of life indicated as a background to the action of his characters. Allusions to Greek history, literature, institutions, topography, social habits are freely combined with Roman details. His auditors would be familiar with most of the Greek topics, and with the Greek language, snatches of which occur now and again. Tranio mentions Philemon and Diphilus by name (*Mos-*

*tellaria* 1149); the Sicilian princes, Agathocles, Hiero, and others are enumerated (*Menaechmi* 409 ff.); a cunning talker is compared to Socrates (*Pseudolus* 465); the Parthenon is mentioned, but as " Minerva's citadel " (*Bacchides* 900 f.). The social atmosphere is usually Athenian: not only do we hear of details like the *agoranomus* (*Captivi* 823) and the *cottabos* (*Trinummus* 1011); the whole morality in most plays is utterly non-Roman. " This is what we are allowed to do in Athens," Stichus explains (446 ff.). Above all, it is astounding to find, in the period of the Punic Wars, Roman plays that speak of war as something remote, an occupation for young men who must seek their fortune or withdraw themselves from an unfortunate love-affair. But Roman details abound also. The *Miles* (164) refers to the gaming law, and in the same play (211 f.) Plautus writes a famous allusion to his illustrious predecessor Naevius, imprisoned for attacks on the Metelli:

*nam os columnatum poetae esse indaudivi barbaro,*
*quoi bini custodes semper totis horis occubant.*

" For I have heard of a barbarian poet whose chin is thus propped upon his hands, while two

[ 26 ]

warders ceaselessly at all hours lie in watch beside him." The Roman influence is at times so strong that we light upon strange juxtapositions, such as aediles and praetors in Athens (*Captivi* 823, *Epidicus* 25). Despite what has been said above about war, the Punic Wars are more than once mentioned (*e.g. Cistellaria* 202), and it may be that *Miles* 219 ff. was meant to arouse a demand that Scipio should be forthwith sent to invade Africa.[34] And despite the prevailing morality we find in *Trinummus* an austere tone which, it has been acutely suggested,[35] shows Plautus vigorously supporting the efforts of Cato the Censor.

It will be remembered that we stigmatized the bulk of Plautine work as very bad, but distinguished perhaps one-seventh of it as excellent. The reason for this abrupt cleavage now grows clear. When the plays are strongly suffused by Plautus' own personality and interests they are mostly deplorable: he is writing in the Atellane manner. When he merely translates, giving little or no admixture of his own material, the result is comparatively good, sometimes splendid, according as the Greek original was merely talented or a work of genius. The result is that we find only one rational principle for discussing his work. The genuinely Greek passages should be distinguished from the far larger bulk where the original has been smothered by barbarous clownery, intolerable verbosity, and an almost complete indifference to dramatic structure. Let us begin with the more welcome task and consider first the Greek element. That consists of one whole play, the *Mercator;* to this might be added various scattered scenes in the other nineteen works, such as the opening conversation in *Pseudolus,* the sea-scenes of the *Rudens,* and parts of the *Miles Gloriosus.* These latter will however most conveniently appear in the course of a general discussion of Plautus' characteristics when we arrive at what we may call the nineteen Roman plays.

that a good number of its companions are worse; and that does not help. There is not even any patching up at the end by means of a discovery that Pasicompsa is a *civis Attica* like the best of them. She and Charinus intend and practise simple cohabitation without apology, regret or misgiving; but we are to remember the important facts that she is very fond of him and that he is passionately devoted to her. Nevertheless, this play was intended by Philemon to please the most thoughtless and self-indulgent among the gilded youth of Athens: that is made abundantly plain by the elaboration of the scene in which Demipho is taken to task and (even more) by the impudent epilogue.

In no sense, save that it is written in Latin, is this a Roman play. Plautus has indeed thrust in a *canticum* (325 ff.) which, though not very bad, nevertheless occasions the one annoying point, namely that Charinus soliloquizes in his father's presence, is however not heard by him, and concludes his self-communing with a startled ejaculation — " But hush! There's Father " precisely as if he had strayed into the *Casina* or the *Poenulus*. Elsewhere Plautus has confined himself to translating, and translating admirably. With little exaggeration we may congratulate ourselves on recovering a whole play of Philemon, and may fancy we understand why even Menander was so often defeated by him. From Menander's not too meagre fragments we gather that he composed high comedy — comedy that contained close thinking about the permanent interests of humanity. Such work demands experience, thought and disciplined emotion in the auditor. Philemon, and no doubt many less distinguished poets of his age, wrote (we gather) charmingly light immoral stuff to last for a glorious hour. Such work is flimsy, referring only to the imagined moment and cannot be thought of in connexion with continuous real life. For example, the *jeune premier* marries in his teens; when his son is ready to become a *jeune premier* in his turn, the father must be under forty; yet every father is called a *senex* (" old man "), and a deplorably obsolete *senex* to boot. Still, such writing can be extremely attractive. At the opening of the *Mercator* Charinus uses a word hardly found elsewhere in Plautus — *elegantia*.[40] That is perhaps the greatest charm of this comedy: elegance. It is buoyant, rapid, clear, sparkling in plot, dia-

[ 38 ]

logue and situations — a welcome patch of sunlight in the fog.

Let us consider first the plot. Here are no
lagoons of irrelevant jest, no stumbling bac-
chiacs to proclaim in endless platitudes the importance of being earnest. Even if we apply
the severest standards of construction we shall
find little to blame. It has already been
mentioned that a *canticum* causes a creak in
the machinery. Further, when Demipho and
Charinus unconsciously reassure one another
(380 ff.), the situation is delightful, but it has
to be pointed by two sets of asides. Again, to
save Charinus (and the audience) the trouble
of an explanation to Eutychus, he is made to
hear the whole story from the portico (477).
One passage is certainly intrusive — the soliloquy (817–829) wherein Syra laments the
"double law":

*nam si vir scortum duxit clam uxorem suam,*
*id si rescivit uxor, inpunest viro;*
*uxor virum si clam domo egressa est foras,*
*viro fit caussa, exigitur matrumonio.*

"If a husband takes a courtesan without his
wife's knowledge, and the wife discovers it, the
husband goes scot-free. But if a wife without

her husband's knowledge walks abroad, the husband has a grievance and she is divorced." This looks like an insertion by Plautus of a striking passage in Menander's *Arbitration*. It can hardly have belonged to Philemon's play. Lysimachus at any rate is being punished by Dorippa's anger and reproaches; above all, she sends for her father, which certainly means that she contemplates his transferring herself and her dowry from Lysimachus' control to his own.

Every entrance and exit, every conversation, is dramatically accounted for instead of being flung at the audience casually. When we see Lysimachus allowing Demipho the use of his house because his wife is out of town, we know that she will duly appear; but she gives a reason,[41] though it is (as the novelists say) a woman's reason. The poet has two excellent but different ideas for Charinus' speech of departure. Each is too good to throw away, and he contrives to use both by a perfectly sound device — Eutychus' reluctance to take his friend indoors while his mother is so distressed. Again, the superb farce of the cook's scene (741–782) is introduced with perfect skill: he comes because he has been summoned; and he has been summoned for a reason essential to the plot. But might not a strict investigator assert that the scene (499–543), in which Lysimachus brings Pasicompsa to his house, is intrusive — that it could be excised with no damage to the plot? The passage is (in the strictest possible sense) unneeded, for the mechanism would be uninjured were it to vanish. But it helps us to enjoy, perhaps to understand, the whole better. First, it is the one scene in which Pasicompsa appears. Secondly, she is seen weeping for her lover and proclaims that she is devoted to him. Thirdly, we realize what is afoot when we actually see her conducted into the house: we know of this, to be sure, but it is interesting to watch. Fourthly, this scene gives occasion once more for the unconscious prophecy of Dorippa's invasion: "my wife is not at home." Mechanically, the scene is useless; artistically it helps a great deal.

Otherwise the construction is perfect: each part, sound and interesting in itself, has an organic relation to other parts. The "question of the play" is: Can the youth keep his mistress in peace now that his father knows of her presence? The solution is: By discomfiting him so ignominiously that he is only too glad to acquiesce. The dénouement is the establishment of Charinus, and promulgation of a " law " in favour of persons like him and in repression of persons like Demipho. The solution is Eutychus' discovery that the girl in Lysimachus' house is the missing Pasicompsa. Eutychus discovers this because he enters the house; he enters because his parents have quarrelled; they have quarrelled because of Pasicompsa's presence; she is there, and not elsewhere, because Demipho wishes to keep her for himself; he wishes this because he saw her on the ship; and that is the very event that brought about the " question of the play." The difficulty itself brings about its own solution. The *Mercator* is a small piece of machinery, but it is beautifully conceived.

So much for the plot. Characterization, properly so called, there is none: Philemon was clearly a dramatist of situations, not of characters. But the style and the conduct of the scenes are both delightful.

Admirable jokes and repartees abound. When the Cook, whose untimely arrival agonizes Lysimachus, is told to go away he exclaims (750): " Aren't you going to have

PLAUTUS: MERCATOR

any dinner? " Lysimachus feelingly answers:
" We've had enough already " (*iam saturi su-
mus*).  When Charinus, eager to rejoin his beloved, is told (373) that he looks pale and
ought to " go and lie down " he insists that he
has to finish certain affairs entrusted to him,
" and they *must* come first."  Later, seeing that
his father is off to the Piraeus in order to sell
the girl, he offers to accompany him, but is
silenced by a reminder (463) that he has affairs entrusted to him, " and they *must* come
first."  As elsewhere, we meet direct allusions
to the theatre.  Charinus tells Acanthio that
he must talk quietly.  " Afraid to wake the
audience? " asks the other (160).[42]  At the
close, when Eutychus suggests that the conversation should be continued indoors, Demipho
agrees (1007): " Excellent!  That will make
the play shorter."  When Demipho is eager to
purchase Pasicompsa for his imaginary friend,
there arise excellent repartees.  " You answer
before I ask."  " Yes, father; and you buy
before I sell " (456).  When Eutychus inquires
how the money needed for the girl's rescue is
to be found, Charinus wildly answers (488):
" I'll ask Achilles for the gold wherewith Hector was weighed."  The other cries " Are you

[ 43 ]

sane? " He replies: " Jove! If I were sane, I should not consult you as a physician." It is pleasantly double-edged. Even more delicious is the close of Demipho's soliloquy. He has dreamed that he entrusted a beautiful she-goat to a monkey and that a kid took her away. He realizes that the she-goat is Pasicompsa but cannot imagine (270) who the kid and the monkey are. Next moment out steps old Lysimachus, looking (why not?) just like a monkey: in any case, he is to be Demipho's confidant, like the monkey. It recalls Blake's couplet:

> A *petty sneaking knave I knew* —
> O! *Mr. Cromek, how do ye do?*

But apart from jokes and repartees, the whole comedy radiates the charm that resides in a perfect mastery of expression: *id iam lucrumst quod vivis* (553) — how clumsily we translate this! " At your time of life it is a gain that you are alive at all." Consider the firm clear diction of the prologue:

> *duas res simul nunc agere decretumst mihi:*
> *et argumentum et meos amores eloquar.*
> *non ego item facio ut alios in comoediis*

*vi vidi amoris facere, qui aut Nocti aut Dii*
*aut Soli aut Lunae miserias narrant suas.*

" Two things at once I have decided to do now:
I will expound the argument and my own love.
I will not act as I have seen others act in
comedies under the power of love, men who
relate their woes to Night or Day or Sun or
Moon." The utter sophistication of these last
three lines! He goes on to explain his repudia-
tion of such appeals: these deities care nothing
for human lamentations. He is preaching
Epicureanism, a system inaugurated at Athens
in Philemon's lifetime. Such views, voiced at
this date in Rome, have a completely exotic
air. This impression is reinforced by other
Athenian touches — the allusion to the *peplos*
of Athena (67) and to Greek literature earlier
than Philemon. Such things are frequent in
the other plays, the most striking instance being the too long but vigorous parody of the
Trojan War in *Bacchides* (925 ff.); but in the
*Mercator* they are not cheek by jowl with Roman ideas. Charinus, as we saw, quotes (488)
the story that Hector's body was redeemed for
its weight in gold. Later he delivers a parody
— or, rather, a touching imitation (931 ff.) —

[ 45 ]

of some passage in a Greek tragedy: it re-
minds us of Heracles' frenzy [48] and somewhat
of Hippolytus' farewell; [44] but it is most probably based by Philemon upon some drama,
now lost, concerning Teucer's banishment to
Cyprus.[45] While we are considering literary
parallels we may fancy we detect two passages
that clung to Shakespeare's memory. Polonius'
invitation, "Take this from this, if this be
otherwise," is like *decide collum stanti si fal-
sum loquor* (308); and when the distraught
lover cries (471 ff.):

*cur ego vivo? cur non morior? quid mihist in vita
    boni?*
*certumst, ibo ad medicum atque ibi me toxico morti
    dabo,*
*quando id mi adimitur qua caussa vitam cupio
    vivere,*

we are put in mind of Romeo's visit to the
Mantuan apothecary. "Why do I live? Why
not death? What profit have I in life? I will
to the physician's and there with poison deal
myself death, since that is torn from me which
makes me desire life."

Three scenes are especially notable for spar-
kle and vigour, Philemon being (as we said)

PLAUTUS: MERCATOR

a playwright of situation rather than of characters.

The first is the laughable sham-auction, which contains an extraordinarily vivid bit of imaginative writing. Demipho points out that Pasicompsa is too lovely and elegant to be a success as his wife's handmaid (402 ff.):

> illa forma matrem familias
> flagitium sit si sequatur; quando incedat per vias,
> contemplent, conspiciant omnes, nutent, nictent,
>     sibilent,
> vellicent, vocent, molesti sint, occentent ostium:
> impleantur elegeorum meae fores carbonibus.

"It would be a scandal for such a beauty to attend a matron. When she walked down the street, all the men would gaze and stare — nodding, winking, whistling, nudging, calling, jostling, singing at the gate! My doors would be covered with charcoal sonnets."

Next comes the delicious farce of the cook-scene (741 ff.). Dorippa suddenly returns, finds the girl, and furiously taxes her husband with infidelity. Just as he is doing his very bad best to hum and ha his way out of this scrape, the Cook arrives at the head of his assistants, carrying gear for Demipho's ban-

quet. This man has been hired by Lysimachus,
who now in anguish bids him go. The Cook
cannot understand, and when Dorippa intervenes, he blandly turns to Lysimachus: " Is
this the little lady you told me you were in
love with? " Despite frenzied appeals he
passes on to compliments — " a dainty bit "
(*satis scitum filum mulieris*), and the like.
Lysimachus then attempts to deny that he is
the man who engaged the Cook, but that per-
sistent artist proves his point. " Oh, come!
You're the man himself. You know — your
wife is in the country: you hate her like a
snake, you said." Lysimachus frantically re-
pudiates such views. But Dorippa intervenes:
" No! All this proves that you hate me."
The Cook blandly tries to soothe her. " Oh,
no! It wasn't you he said he hated, but his
wife." Even before an experienced audience
at the Palais Royal this scene would be a
*succès fou;* in Athens it may well have brought
Philemon one of those prizes for which Menander told him he should blush; in Rome its
reception was no doubt mixed.

Our third scene belongs to a kind less
familiar on any stage — a superb piece of romantic comedy: passion, rhetoric and poetry

entwined with perfect delicacy of touch as they
hover on the very edge of the ludicrous — a
rainbow dancing above the abyss. Such is the
Farewell of Charinus in the Fifth Act.

The diction is powerful, coloured, amazingly
clear-cut; the nimble fiery rhythm gradually
gathers speed and sweeps the reader along bil-
lows of emotion. It begins, however, calmly:
Charinus speaks with the quietness of despair:

*Limen superum inferumque, salve, simul autem*
*vale:*
*hunc hodie postremum extollo mea domo patria*
*pedem.*
*usus, fructus, victus, cultus iam mihi harunc aedium*
*interemptust, interfectust, alienatust — occidi!*
*di penates meum parentum, familiai Lar pater,*
*vobis mando meum parentum rem bene ut tutemini.*

"Threshold and lintel, hail; and in the same
breath farewell! In this hour I step forth from
my father's house for the last time. The sweet
usages of my home, in life's plainer modes and
deeper influences, are now for me destroyed
and slain. I am a stranger here, a man that
once was. Household gods of my father and
my mother, and the Guardian-Spirit of this
family, thy children, to you I entrust my par-

[ 49 ]

ents' fortunes. Protect them well." From the
other house Eutychus bursts forth in a rapture
of relief, but Charinus is absorbed in his grief
and goes on with rising pain: now he is
equipped for his wanderings, all pride flung
away. But this is no tragic drama: quaintly
he enumerates the different functions that he
must himself fulfil since his stern humility
brooks no company — "I am my own companion, lackey and horse: my own groom and
armour-bearer." Such self-confidence has he
found in his passion — *O Cupido, quantus es!*
One thought governs his grief-obscured brain,
and his voice rises to the height of his solitary
heart-broken search for her he loves:

*certa rest*

*me usque quaerere illam quoquo hinc abductast*
*gentium;*
*neque mihi ulla opsistet amnis nec mons neque adeo*
*mare*
*nec calor nec frigus metuo neque ventum neque*
*grandinem;*
*imbrem perpetiar, laborem sufferam, solem, sitim;*
*non concedam neque quiescam usquam noctu neque*
*dius*
*priu' profecto quam aut amicam aut mortem*
*investigavero.*

This is the true romantic passion, the death-less ardour that was to flame up again in *Manon Lescaut*. " My purpose is fixed. Al-ways will I seek her, to whatever spot of earth she has been led from me. No river shall bar my path, no mountain — no, nor sea. No heat or frost, no tempest or hail shall affright me. Rain and weariness, sun and thirst, I will bear and outface. No yielding, no rest by day or night — never, until my search leads to my darling or to death! " And last, as he turns to his quest, the voice of his friend breaks into his consciousness:

Eu.             *ilico*
     *sta, Charine.*
Ch.          *quis me revocat?*
Eu.                     *spes, salus, victoria.*

How the voice rises to that triumphant *victoria!* Then comes a neat little jest to relieve the strain. Charinus answers " What do you want? " We, of course, knowing that one per-son addresses him, expect *quid me vis?* But he says *quid me voltis*, wildly believing that Hope, Rescue, and Victory are three goddesses calling him. Eutychus advances and soothes him in strangely beautiful language: he must

[ 51 ]

turn round and come back home, for out yonder is threatening weather and here the breeze
is calm:

*hic favonius serenust, istic auster imbricus . . .*
*caelum ut est splendore plenum nonne ex advorso*
    *vides?*

This is poetry: the words, whether lovely or
not in themselves, draw magic from the situation wherein they and the speaker are placed.
This is one of those moments when it seems
that a writer cannot fail, because he has attained a region whose air is beauty. Then follows a quieter interlude while Charinus is
persuaded that his beloved is at hand. But
Eutychus hesitates to take him into the house
at the moment, because Dorippa is deeply distressed. Charinus imagines himself deceived:
it must be a lie — she is gone after all. This
supposed disillusionment drives him for the
moment utterly mad. Quivering, panting, he
rages to and fro, in fancy urging his search
through the world for his lost love and asking
those he meets where she is to be found — a
marvellous blend of beauty, pathos, and ab-
surdity. Then, his mood abating, he is " home
again from exile " and greets Eutychus with a

[ 52 ]

painful forced urbanity. Following his friend
and rescuer he hastens within, and the peerless
scene closes.

In good hour Plautus has pursued the only
path whereby marked success was for him at-
tainable. Molière was great enough really to
remodel what he took over from an alien dramatist.[46] Plautus was not: here, and here alone,
he kept his appropriate function and was splen-
didly rewarded, though he seems not to have
known it. His own favourite plays were the
patch-work *Pseudolus,* the deplorable *Truculentus* and *Epidicus.*[47] But that matters little:
there is abundant evidence that he could not
distinguish a fine play from a bad. We may be
grateful that he for once made little attempt
to meddle, but, by merely translating — and
translating superbly — allowed the ghost of an
admirable poet to speak through him in still-
living tones.

# IV. PLAUTUS: THE OTHER
## NINETEEN PLAYS

I N THE second chapter we offered a preliminary account of Plautus, which ended
with the statement that his twenty surviving plays must be divided into two categories:
"Greek" work and "Roman." The former is
nearly filled by a single comedy, the *Mercator*.
Other passages that reveal the Greek manner
will be most conveniently mentioned by way of
variety or relief to what we are now to say of
the Roman work.

Any playwright's quality depends upon four
elements: theme, plot-construction, characterization, and verbal style (including dialogue).
With the first we have already dealt. We have
remarked on his lyrical passages also. Many
writers [48] have laid great stress on the fact that
Plautus was a lyrist as well as a playwright:
it is sometimes implied that he was not so
much a playwright at all as a master of musical
comedy. There is no doubt that he gave great
attention to the libretto, the music and the

rendering of solos. Their elaboration, length, and frequency are as noticeable as anything else in his work. But, since we possess nothing save the words, we may consider these *cantica* incidentally to our treatment of other features.

Concerning characterization, too, we may be brief; for, strictly speaking, it is hardly to be discovered in Plautus. All writers are competent to spell social facts or moral qualities with a capital letter and then assign words or actions to these phantoms. Freedom, who "shrieked when Kosciusko fell," "the Passions, a terrific band," "Melancholy, heavenly Maid," are all cut to this pattern. A further stage of proficiency is reached by those who excite our interest in their imagined people, though for so long only as they appear and in connexion only with the immediate situation. To this class belong Virgil's Aeneas and Shakespeare's Julius Caesar. The third kind is genuine creation, whereby genius projects a man or woman authentically alive. The test of success is simple: do we naturally, or with small effort, imagine the person acting in situations other than those set before us by the writer? Homer's Achilles and Nausicaa, Shakespeare's Cleopatra and Falstaff, Dickens' Micawber and

Tony Weller, leap at once to the mind. They
live in three dimensions and are capable of
stepping forth from the page into new enter-
prises, unnarrated calamities. It is no discredit to Plautus that he has produced nothing
like this; but even in the second class whereof
we spoke his achievement stands very low. All
his lovers, heroines, slaves, fathers, parasites,
and pandars are alike, differing only in what
happens to them, not in what they are. Sele-
nium in the *Cistellaria* has charm derived from
some dignity and candour; but how is she distinguished from Philematium in the *Mostellaria?* Ballio in *Pseudolus* stands out only by
his racy vigour of language, Ampelisca and
Palaestra in the *Rudens* only by the pathetic
charm of their plight. There are but two ex-
ceptions: Periplectomenus in the *Miles* not
only gives a vivid description of his own character: we see that character brought to bear
on the intrigue. Euclio in the *Aulularia* is excellent: Plautus has given a fine study of a
man hag-ridden by the sudden discovery of a
buried treasure. This play inspired Molière's
*L'Avare:* there are reminiscences of it in Shakespeare too. Euclio's outburst (713 ff.) when
his money has been stolen recalls famous

speeches of Harpagon and of Shylock; his *dis-crucior animi, quia ab domo abeundum est mihi* (105) — " it is a torment to me that I must leave the house " — cannot fail to remind us of the Jew and Bassanio's invitation.

The other two topics, literary manner (including dialogue) and plot-construction, call for lengthier examination.

First, then, his language. We modern students, for good reasons, come to Plautus only after some reading of Caesar, Livy, Ovid, Horace, and Virgil. His style therefore strikes us as merely hideous: when it is not battering us about the head, it is setting our teeth on edge. He wishes to say " She's as pretty as a picture," and he writes (*Epidicus* 624):

*estne consimilis quasi quom signum pictum pulchre aspexeris?*
" Is she not like as when you have looked at a picture prettily painted? "

Again: " A man like this master of mine " (*Poenulus* 824):

*quoi homini erus est consimilis velut ego habeo hunc huiusmodi.*
" A man to whom is a master similar like as I have this of this kind."

[ 57 ]

Again: " Follow duty, not self-indulgence "
(*Trinummus* 311):

*nimio satiust ut opust ted ita esse quam ut animo
lubet.*
" It is better by far to be thus, as it is needful that
you should be, than as it is agreeable to your
temper."

Or, to select longer passages, we first listen to
the music of the *Eclogues* and then find this
(*Menaechmi* 571 ff.) bumping against our ears:

*ut hoc utimur maxime more moro,
molesto atque multo atque uti quique sunt
optumi maxime morem habent hunc!
clientes sibi omnes volunt esse multos:
bonine an mali sint, id hau quaeritant; res
magis quaeritur quam clientum fides
quoiusmodi clueat.*

This incredible solo staggers on for many lines
more, but throws up nothing to surpass that
exquisite bacchius *habent hunc*. When we thus
pass from Virgil to Plautus, we may well con-
ceive that we are prowling in the slums of
literature. But our modern way of approach to
him, though excusable in those learning Latin
as a foreign tongue, is irrational. Six genera-

tions of deepening scholarship, of splendid and
sustained effort by writers of genius, stretch
between the Latin of the *Menaechmi* and the
Latin of the *Eclogues*. The language grew
from a dialect of creaks, grunts and thuds
only by degrees to a superb instrument of majesty, significance, flexible charm. While we
recognize that the verbal style of Plautus is on
the whole wretched — and no historical con-
siderations can do away with the fact, however
they excuse it — let us be grateful for the effective passages that dart a twinkle through
the gloom. Here, for instance, clearness, vigour, and dignity begin to break through the
spluttering gawkiness of the earlier diction
(*Trinummus* 485 ff.):

*semper tu hoc facito, Lesbonice, cogites,*
*id optumum esse tute uti sis optumus;*
*si id nequeas, saltem ut optumis sis proxumus.*
*nunc condicionem hanc, quam ego fero et quam*
*        abs te peto,*
*dare atque accipere, Lesbonice, te volo.*
*di divites sunt, deos decent opulentiae*
*et factiones, verum nos homunculi*
*scintillula animai, quam quom extemplo emisimus,*
*aequo mendicus atque ille opulentissimus*
*censetur censu ad Acheruntem mortuos.*

" Be sure you always remember, Lesbonicus, it is best that you should be best; and if you cannot, that you should at any rate be closest to the best. Today I wish, Lesbonicus, to give, and I wish you to accept, this match that I offer and that I seek from you. The gods are wealthy, to the gods riches and social advancement rightly belong; but we poor little human creatures are a tiny spark of life, and the moment we have breathed it forth, the beggar and yon prince of wealth are rated in the same class by Acheron's bank in death."

Between the fourth and the last two lines there is a notable difference not only in tone but also in the handling of words. It is tempting but manifestly dangerous to suppose that the earlier half of this passage is free composition. That the latter half is close translation can scarcely be questioned: the commonplace yet moving idea, the quiet dignified pathos of its expression, are exactly like a good many of the fragments that survive from Menander, Philemon, and their fellows. Indeed, if those Plautine passages are scrutinized that combine graceful moralizing with clear and agile diction, it will invariably be found that they are commonplaces, in the original sense of that word: they have no necessary connexion with the dramatic situation wherein they are uttered. It will also be found that they have no specifically Roman quality in language or reference. The natural assumption is that he is closely translating. Similar passages to this of the *Trinummus* are Periplectomenus' description (*Miles* 627 ff.) of himself as an elderly man of the world, the bright and graceful opening of *Pseudolus* where Calidorus discusses his love-affairs with his confidential slave, and that little sermon (*Rudens* 1235 ff.) on the temptations of avarice which so plainly reveals its Greek origin that Macaulay was impelled to translate it back again.[49]

It naturally results that few passages of Plautus haunt either heart or brain. Nevertheless he does now and again write well in his own person; this may be quoted, from a *canticum*, of all unlikely places (*Curculio* 147 ff.):

> *pessuli, heus pessuli, vos saluto lubens,*
> *vos amo, vos volo, vos peto atque opsecro,*
> *gerite amanti mihi morem, amoenissumi,*
> *fite caussa mea ludii barbari,*
> *sussilite, opsecro, et mittite istanc foras*
> *quae mihi misero amanti ebibit sanguinem.*

[ 61 ]

It is a serenade. " Ye bolts, hola! Ye bolts,
you I greet gladly; you I love, you I seek and
implore. Indulge a lover, you delightful creatures. For my sake become barbarian dancers
and leap, I pray: let her out of doors who
drinks the blood of this hapless loving heart."
The merits of this song are modest; but there
is some intelligence behind it, the expression
is lucid, and the repetitions are for once explained by the subject-matter.

In his management of long passages the
same variety may be discerned, though we
cannot attribute it entirely to the same reasons.
Most are dull, laboured, stuffed with fumbling
repetitions; a few are excellent. We may instance Ballio's racy address to his troop of
slaves (*Pseudolus* 133 ff.), the curious, satiri-
cal 'guide-book to Rome' that is suddenly
dragged into *Curculio* (466–486), and the vivid
description of a wreck in the *Rudens* (152 ff.)
— *homunculi quanti estis! eiecti ut natant!* is
a good sample: " In they go! How they swim!
Bravo, you little beggars! " It is perhaps to
scenes like these, and to the rattle of expletives
in the frequent interchanges of abuse, that Horace alludes when he writes that Plautus has
speed.[50] The bad passages are far more fre-

quent. In the *Captivi*, the need to see that the prisoners do not escape is propounded with ridiculous elaboration, the climax being Hegio's elephantine epigram (255 f.):

*qui cavet ne decipiatur vix cavet quom etiam cavet;*
*etiam quom cavisse ratus est saepe is cautor captus est.*

" He who takes precautions lest he be deceived is scarcely taking them even when he is taking them; even when he has thought he has taken them, often that taker of precautions is caught." But the *Captivi*, as we shall see later, outdoes all its companions in sheer blockhead-edness. Further examples need not be dissected: it is enough to mention the *Asinaria*, where a simple and age-old swindle is discussed and guffawed over till we begin to wonder whether there will be room in the play for anything else, and the incessant sermonizing in *Truculentus* about wasting one's substance on courtesans — it is very good advice, but we feel after a time that the verb *pereo* is only less frequent than *sum* itself.

Despite adverse stars, Plautus is sometimes amusing, and that though we are restricted to his words and can but feebly imagine what his

scenes must have been as spectacles. Puns
are found, such as *Persa* and *persona* (*Persa*
783), *eira, ira,* and *era* (*Truculentus* 264), a
purely Greek pun (*Bacchides* 240) — *opus est
chryso Chrysalo* — and a Latin joke on a Greek
name (*ib.* 284 f.). There are some good plays
on words. Tranio says (*Mostellaria* 427 ff.):

> *ludos ego hodie vivo praesenti hic seni
> faciam, quod credo mortuo numquam fore.*

" I will today make game of my old master as
he stands here alive — he will certainly have
no games when he is dead." The fun depends
on two meanings of *ludi:* " trickery," and
" games in honour of the dead." Wit at times
flashes out: " I believe you when you say you
are his servant, because you tell lies " (*Curculio* 452). In *Pseudolus* (974 ff.) Simo explains: " I'm looking for a man about here —
a knavish criminal heartless perjured scoundrel." Ballio at once remarks: " It's me he
wants." Unfortunately Plautus murders the
joke by going on to explain it.[51] " For those
are all titles of mine. If only he would mention the name! What is the man's name? "
Then he is told " Ballio," and we can all burst
into a hearty (if belated) laugh. Certain good

[ 64 ]

remarks, naturally, cannot be appreciated without a large context, like *semel bibi* (*Rudens* 884) and Curculio's *nihil attuli* (327). This latter is the climax of a capital scene, closely resembling that where Juliet's Nurse postpones announcement of her tidings by the complicated distress due to her hurry in bringing it.[52] A pretended madman delivers a good parody of tragic ravings (*Menaechmi* 862 ff.), one line of which has that rarest of Plautine effects, good clear rhythm:

*cursu celeri facite inflexa sit pedum pernicitas.*
" Fleetly flying, nimbly bounding, speed your
    hooves in full career."

It seems reasonable to credit most of the impropriety in these plays to the Greek originals. Aristotle [53] remarks that later comedy preferred innuendo to frank indecency; and we can see for ourselves (so far as the fragments allow) that Middle and New dramatists avoided obscene language though they presented situations the whole matter of which was immoral, perhaps downright corrupting. Exactly the same is true of Plautus, save in *Casina*. Not only do most of his works rest on sexual irregularity that is at least condoned;

some are utterly depraved in temper. Nevertheless, verbal indecency is very rare. But a further remark seems needed. Indecency is not of one kind only, or of two. In particular it is possible to be indelicate gracefully and also disgustingly: in other words, we may or may not add sins of taste to offences against ethics. More than once Plautus carries bad taste to the pitch of infamy. The *Amphitruo* has been briefly mentioned. Whether it is really worse than the close of the *Asinaria* may be doubted. There we find a lecherous old man joining his son and his son's mistress at their revel. The conversation turns on his wife and her failings as compared with the courtesan's merits; the son asks — let us translate this carefully — " I say, father, do you love mother at all? " (*Quid ais, pater? ecquid matrem amas?* 899 f.). That the wife is listening unseen, and presently hales her husband ignominiously away, adds nothing to the achievement, for it cannot receive increase. It is difficult to believe that Plautus is alone responsible for this monstrosity, or that Demophilus, the Greek who wrote his original, *The Wild Ass,* was alone responsible either; such a triumph seems to demand the co-operation of giants.

The truth is, the extreme of indecorum is reached only when decadence or corruption appropriate to one environment is forcibly transferred to another. We can believe that what Demophilus wrote was corrupt but had some saving grace of gallantry or wit; that Plautus, if writing for himself, would have blent with his grossness some memory that he was a human being. Unfortunately he took a passage only just possible in the language and the life of a decadent, utterly sophisticated, people and translated it into a rougher language forged and used by a race crude in sentiment, ignorant of subtleties.

We have now to deal with plot-construction, the most fundamental task of any playwright.

In his expositions Plautus composes not only the normal preliminary scenes but (usually) a prologue also. This element has had a varied history. First it was, as Aristotle [54] defines it, merely that part of a tragedy which precedes the first song of the whole chorus: the prologue might be a conversation, a monologue, a song divided between individual choristers, or a combination of all these; and some tragedies had no prologue at all. A development here, as in so many other things, was made by

Euripides, who began to throw this introductory scene into an undisguised explanatory address delivered by one of the characters. Thus the *Phoenissae* opens with a business-like speech by Jocasta, telling the history of Oedipus' family and the recent events that have brought about the situation now to be developed. Aristophanes takes over this method: Strepsiades in the *Clouds* is the exact analogue of Jocasta. Later comedians introduced a remarkable extension of this: their prologues not only put the spectator *au fait,* but also revealed the plot that was now to be unfolded. We should today think this a disastrous and gratuitous blemish. But, firstly, the ancient comedy of manners usually handled (as we have seen) the same kind of story, so that the surprise-interest was in any case weaker than it is now; secondly, ancient spectators were at least as concerned to discover how a result, known or not, was achieved, as to learn the result itself. Plautus inherits this type of prologue — an introductory address that tells the plot. Terence never employs it for this purpose, but always confines it to discussion of his own methods, censure of his critics, and the like; this has been the function of the prologue (and the epilogue) in modern plays, though during recent years there has grown up a custom of writing a prologue that is merely the first scene of the play proper.

Not all the existing Plautine prologues were written by the poet himself: some were composed for revivals produced after his death. The prologue of *Casina* tells us this in so many words: "Since we gather from common talk that you earnestly desire Plautine dramas, we have produced an old comedy of his that won the approval of you older people." But most of the prologues are no doubt the poet's own work. They are in the main dull, though easily understood. Indeed one feature of them is the extraordinary repetitions: there was so much noise from those already seated and from latecomers, that he finds it necessary to tell them again and again whose son was kidnapped, and when. "Do you grasp this now? Excellent! Ah, a gentleman at the back says he doesn't. Come forward! If there is no place for you to sit, there is room for you to walk away, since you force an actor to become a beggar" (*Captivi* 10 ff.). Very rarely we find admirable writing. The *Rudens* begins with these attractive lines:

*qui gentis omnis mariaque et terras movet,*
*eiius sum civis civitate caelitum.*
*ita sum ut videtis splendens stella candida,*
*signum quod semper tempore exoritur suo*
*hic atque in caelo: nomen Arcturo est mihi.*
*noctu sum in caelo clarus atque inter deos,*
*inter mortales ambulo interdius.*

"That god who wields all nations, seas and lands — his subject am I in the heavenly city. Thus am I, as you see, a star of dazzling whiteness, that rise always at the due season here and in heaven. My name is Arcturus. By night I glitter in heaven amid the gods; by day I walk among mankind."

Such a method of imparting antecedent facts is of course mechanical. A far better plan is to work such information into the body of the play, of which method the most perfect model is Ibsen's *Rosmersholm,* where indeed recollection and revelation are the very stuff of the action; a less subtle, but still excellent, example is Sophocles' *Oedipus Tyrannus.* Towards this a slight advance was made early. Alexis in one at least of his works postponed the prologue (if the name is still legitimate) till after the first stage of the action; his nephew and pupil Menander did the same in his *Hero* and *The*

*Shorn Lady.* So does Plautus now and again. The *Cistellaria* has a prologue delivered by ' Auxilium ' at the close of the first act. In the *Miles,* too, it is given late, and by a person of the play, Palaestrio. The *Trinummus* prologue tells us (16 f.): " Do not expect me to give the argument of the play: the old men who will come here will open the business to you ":

> *sed de argumento ne exspectetis fabulae:*
> *senes qui huc venient, i rem vobis aperient.*

*Amphitruo* has two prologues — a very long and wretchedly bad passage at the beginning, probably not by Plautus, and a later prophetical and business-like address (473 ff.); both are delivered by the god Mercury. Not satisfied with this, the playwright offers us a third harangue (861 ff.) by Jupiter himself.

Prologue and explanatory scenes alike contribute to the first great element in dramatic structure: the promulgation of the " question of the play." This is as a rule satisfactorily done by Plautus: we know what is afoot. But so much is to be found in nearly all plays. Excellence here consists in a good deal more — in so stating the problem that the solution is inherent therein. That is, the solution, though it may surprise, should not seem unnatural: the exposition should contain the ingredients of the solution. Sudden incursions, towards the close, of " the god from the machine " are thoroughly bad, in whatever disguise he appears — the sudden rich uncle, or the man who happened to witness the murder but has not seen the newspapers till this morning. Here Plautus is far less good. Moreover, he commits the converse fault of sending out for exposition-purposes people who will not appear again. In the *Mostellaria* we learn the situation from a quarrel between Tranio and Grumio after which the latter disappears for good. Similar " characters " are found in the *Cistellaria, Curculio, Epidicus,* even the *Mercator;* they were called by the Greek critics *protatica prosopa* (" introductory characters "). This crude device is extraordinarily favoured by dramatists of widely-sundered ages. In fact the explanatory domestic (" Did you hear the master and mistress quarrelling last night? " "What! Has he been gambling again? Let me tell you . . .") is the most long-lived of all dramatic characters: he arrives in Euripides' *Medea* (431 B.C.) and is still flourishing in

Mr. Shaw's *Apple-Cart* (A.D. 1929). Certainly Plautus sins in good company.

Passing now to development, the conflict and co-operation of the characters whereby the solution is attained, we come upon a great and most important perplexity. There are quite a number of good things — some very good — and many bad. Nor is this jumble a contrast only between separate works: the astonishing fact is that the jumble often occurs inside one play. It is due to his curious notion of a Roman dramatist's function. Sometimes he will merely translate a Greek scene; at other times he will write a scene wholly or largely original; the matter thus produced he will heap together in a merely chronological order; now and again he will enlarge the pile by putting in scenes from some other play than his first original. Let us begin by studying the scenes themselves, passing later to their combination.

Excellent scenes are found. The *Aulularia* contains a capital conversation at cross-purposes (731 ff.), when Lyconides is talking of a woman, Euclio about his pot of gold, and each (misled by the feminine genders employed) supposes that the other is talking of the same subject as himself. In *Bacchides* a letter abusing Chrysalus is dictated (728 ff.) by Chrysalus himself for a trick. In the *Miles,* the heroine pretends to be her own twin-sister by appearing alternately on the roofs of adjacent houses. The *comissatio* of Callidamates (*Mostellaria* 313 ff.), where the youth reels along with his mistress Delphium to pay a drunken call on his friend, shows real sprightliness and sound low comedy. *Stichus* has a curiously long elaborate drinking-party (641 ff.) of three slaves, in which the dances and gestures, rather than our worthless lines, must have formed a great attraction: it is probably one of the most Atellane things in Plautus. Let us count it then among the successful scenes. *Amphitruo* contains admirable scenes of bafflement between Mercury and Sosia, indeed — if we can swallow our disgust — between Alcmena and her husband. Mercury, in furtherance of his father's design, takes upon himself the exact likeness of Sosia, Amphitruo's henchman. This leads to irresistible farce: the interview between the two Sosias (the imitation whereof in Molière's play has created the French word for a " double " — *sosie*), and the later scene where the true Sosia insists, to the natural annoyance of Amphitruo, that he met himself and was thrashed by himself. These situations have tempted many playwrights, from Molière himself and Dryden down to the anonymous author of *Jacke Juggler:* M. Jean Giraudoux names his own pungent comedy (produced in 1929) *Amphitryon 38,* and the number may well be correct.

Here are to be added those Greek passages that we mentioned briefly when describing the *Mercator.* The most unmistakable of these occurs in *Bacchides* (925–978), very good though much too long. The contriving valet Chrysalus comes forth to delude his old master Nicobulus and compares the situation elaborately with the siege of Troy: he himself is Ulysses, the deceptive letter is the wooden horse, and so forth. The passage is cleverly worked out and is plainly a close translation of a Greek passage that specially struck Plautus' imagination; otherwise he would not have kept all these detailed identifications with Greek heroes, some at least of whom, such as Epius and Sino, can hardly have touched a chord in many hearts among his audience. Another spirited and witty passage is the list of instructions (*Asinaria* 746 ff.) that Diabolus draws up to govern the behaviour of his mistress — pre-

cautions against even the most rudimentary
flirtation. Nothing could be more plainly New
Comedy: for instance, she is told in Latin that
she is to speak no language except Attic. A
very charming passage opens *Pseudolus,* where
Calidorus shows his slave the letter written by
his mistress, full of passionate love and despair
because she is on the point of being sent away
to the soldier who is purchasing her. Thus we
find ourselves at once embarked on an exciting
plot: can Calidorus and Pseudolus rescue her
in time? The complication begins with no de-
lay and no haste: the very first words of the
play are Pseudolus' inquiry into his master's
trouble. An unforced elegance of style matches
this deftness of manipulation: this scene is perhaps the most Attic passage in Plautus, just as
the harangue of Ballio, which immediately follows, is pre-eminent among his original scenes.
Consider Pseudolus' first speech to Calidorus.
It is unmistakable New Comedy Greek — not
beautiful or pungent, simply urbane and win-
ning. Moreover it seems to contain a reminis-
cence of the admirable prologue to Euripides'
*Iphigenia at Aulis:* [55]

> *si ex te tacente fieri possem certior,*
> *ere, quae miseriae te tam misere macerant,*

[ 76 ]

*duorum labori ego hominum parsissem lubens,*
*mei te rogandi et tis respondendi mihi;*
*nunc quoniam id fieri non potest, necessitas*
*me subigit ut te rogitem. responde mihi:*
*quid est quod tu exanimatus iam hos multos dies*
*gestas tabellas tecum, eas lacrimis lavis*
*nec tui participem consili quemquam facis?*
*eloquere, ut quod ego nescio id tecum sciam.*

" Master, if with no words from you I could
learn what miseries so miserably mangle you,
I should be glad to save two men trouble — me
of asking you and you of answering me. But
since that cannot be, necessity forces me to
question you. Answer me: how is it that for
these many days you have been all distraught,
carrying that letter about, washing it with tears
but making no one a partaker of your thoughts?
Speak, so that I may share in your knowledge
of what I do not know." Nothing here is original Plautus except the jesting alliteration in
the second line. A far finer passage occurs near
the close of *Amphitruo*. The husband's fierce
determination to enter his house and put the
adulterer to the sword even if Jupiter himself
forbids, is met by a crash of thunder that
stretches him senseless upon his own threshold.
Bromia, rushing forth in a rapture of terror and

exaltation, describes the awful glory of light-
ning and thunder that has attended the delivery
of Alcmena. She sees her master prostrate at
her feet and raises him from his stupor to learn
how Heaven brought a painless birth of twins,
one of whom has already given miraculous evidence of his heroic prowess. This is all nobly
written.[56] However deep its debt may be to
Greek, the Latin itself is Plautus' own.

The bad scenes are far more numerous.
Little need be said of those whose badness consists merely in an amazing absence of merit,
such as the absurdly long dull cook-scene in
*Pseudolus* (790–895), the lumbering verbosity
of Megadorus' conversation with his sister
(*Aulularia* 120–177), Antipho's part in *Stichus,*
and practically the whole of the *Persa* and *Truculentus.* There resides a more sinister attractiveness in passages marked by positive rather
than negative faults.

First, dramatic effects are gained by mis-
erable evasions of dramatic method. In
*Bacchides* (573 ff., not a prologue) the parasite
addresses the audience, telling us who and what
kind of man his patron is, and so forth. In
*Casina* (685 ff.) Pardalisca admits us to the
plot by bawling to the audience the following

useful remark, while her dupe stands at her elbow pretending ("by a dramatic convention") not to hear:

> *ludo ego hunc facete;*
> *namque quae facta dixi omnia huic falsa dixi.*

"I am deceiving this man funnily, for all the things that I have told him have occurred, I have told falsely." It may be questioned whether anything else so abject has ever got itself accepted as literature. It is of course plain enough that excellent writers use asides; but there is a vast difference between them, depending on the circumstances. Hamlet's "a little more than kin, and less than kind" is perfect: it might well be uttered in real life; Pardalisca's aside would provoke comment in a madhouse.

We must think much the same of overhearing. No objection can be taken merely because a playwright makes a person overhear a conspiracy and so foil it. But he should observe decency: the plotters must take some precautions. If we are told that, despite this, theatrical conditions compelled Plautus to tell secrets in the street, our answer is obvious. "Unnatural conditions only impose greater care

[ 79 ]

for a decorum of the intelligence. Best of all, if
your plotters must plot in the street, would be
a corresponding convention that they cannot be
overheard, at least not more often or easily
than in a guarded cellar. Still more certainly,
the one chance that plotting in public should
have any verisimilitude is that the conspirators
should never say ' I hope no one is listening.' "
Plautus, oblivious of all, tramps cheerily on,
allowing his private talks to be heard or not
heard just as suits his own comfort. In
*Bacchides* (1104) Philoxenus says " I certainly
thought I heard someone speaking near me."
If Nicobulus' soliloquy is (dramatically) audi-
ble, he is a simpleton to utter it. The *Aulularia*
contains a positively disgraceful instance of
this stupidity. Euclio is hag-ridden by a fear
that someone will discover his treasure; he
therefore removes it from his house to a still
safer place, the temple of Faith. Then he
emerges shouting at the top of his voice
(608 ff.): " O Faith, mind you don't tell anyone that my gold is with you . . . a fine booty
for anyone who found it — a pot full of gold! "
And so forth, with emphatic repetitions. This
is incredible and disgusting enough. But why
not accept this as a stage-convention? How

are we to know what Euclio has done unless we allow him to tell us? Very well: but since he is keeping it a dead secret, this address to Faith should be inaudible save to the spectators. But what happens? Lyconides' slave is secretly listening, and as soon as Euclio departs he promptly exclaims: " Good heavens! What deed have I heard that man describe? He says that he has hidden away a pot of gold . . ." etc. etc. Here Plautus may be seen murdering dramatic art.

If that is the silliest piece of stage-writing in the world, *Casina* runs it close. Lysidamus comes forth into the street, where his wife Cleustrata is standing. He cannot, or does not, see her because it suits the author that he should not. He utters a soliloquy about his love-affair, at the end of which (574 ff.) he sees his wife, again because it suits the author. "But there is my wife in front of the house! Wretched that I am! I fear she is not deaf, but has heard all this." That is, though he now realizes that Cleustrata has heard his so-liloquy, he goes on soliloquizing about her hear-ing it, apparently assuming that Plautus has some mercy and will at least allow these last words of his to escape. Not so. She overhears

[ 81 ]

these words about her overhearing and (not to be outdone) soliloquizes herself: " Oh, yes, I did hear; and you'll regret it." Then laggard convention suddenly jumps back into place. Lysidamus does *not* hear these words of hers, but says — still to himself, old stalwart! — " I'll go up to her," and then, aloud: " How are you, my angel? "

A second weakness is the frequent fumblings — worse still, the padding — whereby development is retarded. Overhearings and cross-overhearings no doubt secure an air of lively bustle; but the activity is usually a sham. Plautus is an ancestor of Mr. Winkle in *The Pickwick Papers* who, being challenged to fight, slowly removed his coat and loudly announced that he was going to begin. Nothing is more frequent than the warning: " But hush! The door is rattling. Someone is coming out." In fact, this same 'Ostium' is a leading Plautine character: small wonder that Phaedromus in *Curculio* (16) inquires after its health! Had it succumbed to the fever, Plautine Comedy would have shared its funeral pyre. Another source of bustle is the running slave. The hero's confidential valet suddenly hears bad news — for instance, that the old master has unexpectedly landed at the Piraeus and will be back home in an hour, as in the *Mostellaria* — and comes hurrying to tell the hero. His arrival makes a favourite scene: he rushes in, proclaiming how breathless he is and how frightfully urgent is his news, yet spends much time on the description of his own collapse, elaborate exhortations to imaginary passers-by to get out of his way, and similar fooleries.[57] As often as not his young master stands attempting in vain to catch his reeling henchman's eye. Of course this brings dramatic action to a standstill, but it must be confessed that here is no bungle. Plautus is quite deliberately shelving the play proper so as to amuse his hearers precisely by ludicrous time-wasting at a crisis. In the *Captivi* this function is filled by the parasite Ergasilus; but parasites are normally used to fetch news or summon guests, and may be called the Plautine equivalent of the telephone. Notwithstanding all this noisy pretence that we are getting on with the play, the action generally proceeds with extreme slowness, only to be dashed through with bewildering speed when we come to the *peripeteia* and dénouement, just as in our musical comedies and the majority of

PLAUTUS AND TERENCE

detective-stories. Time stands still while Philocrates and Tyndarus in the *Captivi* arrange a
plot daring indeed but scarcely subtle, and
while the rascals of the *Asinaria* explain and
re-explain their artless devilry.

Another fault that goes to the very root of
dramatic method is that development itself is
often nerveless: the action advances not so
much because the characters and doings of the
*dramatis personae* clearly make it do so but
because the playwright pushes it. What we
need is machinery that works with a click, and
what we find is manipulation of putty. Satis-
fying crispness of conversation is a necessity of
dramatic development. To offer one specimen
from myriads available: if Mr. Shaw, in *Captain Brassbound's Conversion,* had caused Lady
Cecily gradually to wear down Brassbound's
purpose by perfectly sensible arguments —
" Sir Howard is old, all this happened long ago,
not only you but your followers will probably
be hanged, consider the grief of myself, who
have not wronged you " — he would have been
writing adequate, convincing talk, but not good
drama. What she actually does is first to
startle Brassbound by looking at his mother's
photograph and forcing terrible comment into

[ 84 ]

his mind; next, when he exclaims, at the end of his resources, "There is such a thing as Justice," she rounds on him superbly. "Oh, if you are going to dress yourself up in ermine and call yourself Justice, I give you up. You are just your uncle over again; only he gets £5000 a year for it, and you do it for nothing." That is what we mean by a click: the words "You are just your uncle over again" are not simply adequate: they capture the whole position at a blow and they are magnificently neat. The "click" in dramatic construction corresponds to wit in conversation. This is precisely what Plautus so often fails to execute. Ballio has been deceived by Pseudolus, who sends a man to impersonate Harpax and so get the girl out of Ballio's hands. Later the real Harpax arrives. How is Ballio convinced that this second messenger is the genuine man and that the first was Pseudolus' emissary? By the repeated assertions of Harpax and at length by his description of Pseudolus. This is sound sense, but terribly lacking in crisp precision. So, in the *Trinummus*, the sycophant is convinced that Charmides is Charmides merely by the latter's insistent asseverations.

Perhaps the most effective method by which

Plautus will ruin a scene is suddenly to throw verisimilitude overboard for the sake of a joke or two. The lengths to which he is prepared to go are incredible. In the *Captivi* Hegio is heartbroken by the loss of his son, made prisoner in war; but no sooner does the parasite, who condoles with him, mention eating than this distraught sire perks up his head and dutifully emits a string of jokes and puns about the servants needed to nourish the parasite. In the *Trinummus,* Megaronides begins with a stern soliloquy on the corruption of the age and the rebuke he must deliver to his old friend; but as soon as the friend appears, Megaronides goes off into the familiar blackguardly sneers about his own wife. In the same play Stasimus, the loyal slave grieved by his master's dissipation, changes by miracle into a thieving rascal for a while — *contaminatio* of course, but that is no excuse for Plautus. Trachalio in the *Rudens* acts with the same disregard for sanity, at one time claiming the half of Gripus' find, at another changing his tune altogether. When Ballio is to be cheated, Pseudolus enters with the disguised Simia, and, although the plotters are aware that the genuine envoy may come along at any moment, they waste considerable time in empty quips and boasts (905 ff.). In the *Poenulus,* Hanno has been roaming the world for years in search of his daughters, stolen in childhood. When at last he finds them, before revealing himself he embarks upon an elaborate practical joke, summoning them into the law-court as thieves. Possibly even this atrocity is outdone by the close of the *Rudens,* where the poet's aim is, however, not a joke; what it is, no one knows. The scoundrel Labrax has purchased two little girls and brought them up with a view to prostitution. In the course of the play he cheats the lover of one of them and nearly occasions the death of both by forcing them on shipboard and (as it chances) into a shipwreck. After their escape he persecutes them with ruthless barbarity. But one of them is found to be the daughter of Daemones, who befriends them. At the end, the happiness of father, lover, and daughter is celebrated by a banquet. And Labrax is invited as a guest.

Having examined the quality of separate scenes we pass forward to the next question that we set before ourselves. How are these scenes built together? Is the connexion of cause and effect rational and convincing? Or is it haphazard, a mere tying together of lumps?

In the *Captivi*, Hegio inquires among his other prisoners whether anyone knows Philocrates; thus he finds Aristophontes, who reveals to him that the supposed Philocrates is really the slave Tyndarus, who has by this impersonation contrived the escape of the true Philocrates, his master. But why was Hegio so stupid as not to make this inquiry before he let Philocrates go? Because otherwise the bottom would have dropped out of the plot. Plautus has forced Hegio to act not as suits his obvious interests but as suits a playwright who does not know his business. But there is even worse. The whole activity of Hegio is absurd. Because his son is a prisoner in Elis, he buys up all the Elean prisoners he can, in hopes to find among them one important enough to exchange for his son. Why not simply find out who in Elis holds Philopolemus and send a ransom directly to this person? The elaborate buying up of prisoners is ridiculous: once more, it is a clumsy device to bring in Philocrates and Tyndarus. This fills us with surprised disgust: but soon (334 f.) we learn with stupefaction that Hegio actually knows already the name and profession of the Elean who has purchased his son! Was such a gulf of ineptitude ever plumbed before or since? Nevertheless, this play is incessantly extolled: Sellar [58] places it " among the very best plays of Plautus." The only conceivable explanation of such breath-bereaving judgments is that the morality is unusually high: there is no love-intrigue, and the self-sacrifice of Tyndarus is noble. But that has nothing whatever to do with dramatic excellence. Shall we say that Guido Reni's *Assumption of the Virgin* is a better picture than Titian's *Bacchus and Ariadne* because of the difference in their subjects? Small wonder that Plautus is reputed a good playwright when leaders of criticism and scholarship have adopted standards like this!

Such an exploit is, even in Plautus, unparalleled. But we may find a melancholy spectacle in the *Poenulus*. The scene is laid in Calydon (72,94); later (372) the poet forgets this and makes it Athens; later again (621), he forgets again, and makes it Calydon. Agorastocles the lover burns to purchase Adelphasium's freedom, but fails to keep his promise though the need is urgent, he has plenty of money, and the girl herself reproaches

[ 89 ]

him. Why? We are never told. Here is un-
reason at the very heart of the play. Nor are
these the only absurdities of construction. To
all this the reply is at once given,[59] that the
*Poenulus* is the result of *contaminatio:* Plautus
is combining two Greek plays that refuse to
dovetail. But this is no answer at all. A work
of art is made no better by an exhibition of the
reasons for its badness. The facts are interesting to the historian of literature, but they
diminish in no degree the evidence that Plautus
either does not know, or does not care, what he
is talking about: if he choses to " contaminate,"
he should contaminate like a sane man. But a
quite different excuse has been offered [60] — that
such inconsistencies are not surprising, because
these are mere farces, and Plautus wrote for
people who would only see his work, and see it
but once, not for readers who could examine his
text closely and slowly. This plea, speaking
generally, is sound: it palliates, and in a sense
destroys, most of Aristophanes' mistakes: for
instance the assertion in one passage of the
*Wasps* that Philocleon is toothless, in another
that he bites through his cords.[61] And it may
be held to excuse entirely the wooden construction of the *Pseudolus* in that place (602) where

the slave, instead of thinking out his own plan, jumps at the chance offered by an imbecile who happens to soliloquize. But the excuse will not serve for such crass nonsense as the *Poenulus* and the *Captivi*, unless indeed we are to suppose the audience as indifferent to intellectual decency as the author; and even if it was, that merely shows Plautus to have known his public — it confers no obligation on us to echo their artless plaudits, always supposing they gave any.

For the *Trinummus* we may quote — if only as an indication that we are not interpreting too harshly — the comments of Lejay, a hearty champion of Plautus. "The actions of Callicles are obscure. How can he have installed himself in Charmides' house? Had he no house of his own previously? Does he wish to guard the treasure? Lesbonicus' marriage with his daughter has not been prepared for. The misbehaviour of Lesbonicus has been the subject of allusions only. . . . Plautus must have used abbreviation, especially of the dénouement, over which he is wont to hurry, leaving sidequestions unanswered — whether Charmides will return to his house, whether the riches that he brings home will furnish a dowry,

whether the treasure will be buried again."
Then he gives a broad hint that Philemon, not
Plautus, is to blame for all this! The *Miles*
has two jostling plots, based respectively on
the alleged sister of Philocomasium and on the
alleged wife of Periplectomenus. In *Pseudolus*
the reckless mixture of borrowed intrigues
makes it impossible to understand the com-
plications of Simo and his money. The "structure" of *Casina* is so hopeless as to evade
criticism, but it may be remarked that her supposed madness is later entirely ignored.

Even when the construction is not irrational,
it is childishly obvious. In the *Miles*, Philocomasium has been seen by some slave of the
soldier when she was kissing Pleusicles. The
latter's faithful servant Palaestrio realizes that
this man, whoever he is, will reveal her dis-
loyalty to the soldier, and therefore proposes
(266 ff.) sly detective-work to find who this
hostile witness may be. But no sleuthing is required. Hardly have the words left Palaestrio's lips than out from the soldier's house
steps Sceledrus obligingly talking aloud to himself: "Today I saw Philocomasium looking for
trouble." The lurking detective then subtly
hisses: "He has seen her kissing, to judge by

his words." At a later stage the same fortunate
investigator remarks (1132 ff.): " It would be
useful if at this moment Acroteleutium, or her
maid, or Pleusicles were to come here. Good
heavens! How wonderfully our Lady The-
Nick-Of-Time aids me at every point! The
very persons whom I most desired to see are
coming out before my eyes." And out, in fact,
the three walk, while a myriad Roman eyes
glitter with thrilled amazement. Charmides in
the *Trinummus*, returning home with delight
after long absence and a terrible storm at sea,
stops short (840 ff.) instead of entering his
house because he sees a peculiarly dressed
stranger and is curious to know " what he is
doing here " — really because Plautus needs
his presence.

Now and again the plot-development is emphasized in the last way we should have expected: Plautus makes his people refer to the
play as a play and to themselves as actors.
This is vastly impudent, but the effect is funny
enough. Our best [62] example occurs in the
*Poenulus* (550 ff.) where Agorastocles brings in
the suborned witnesses and is nervous lest they
fail to play their part correctly. They answer:
" All those things we know already, if yonder

[ 93 ]

spectators know: it's for the sake of these spectators that this play is now being acted here. You had better instruct *them,* so that when you perform they may know what you are at. Don't bother about *us.* We know the whole business: of course we learned our parts with you, so that we could give you the proper answers."

It will have been observed that all our examples of construction in the strictest sense, of the building scene upon scene, are to Plautus' discredit. What is there on the other side? Very little, though naturally a course of behaviour promised in one scene is normally followed in some later passage: such a thing is analogous to a "scene," and what we have in mind is rather the growth of a new phase of plot out of an earlier phase. That is where Plautus is weak — save, it must be remembered, in the *Mercator.* All this leads (as we have said before) to a striking conclusion about his dramaturgy, a conclusion to which his practice of *contaminatio* alone might have led us. That is, Plautus' debt to the Greek playwrights consists normally in scenes and scenes alone, not in whole plays. His scenes are good if translated; they are bad (or at least poor)

[ 94 ]

if they are original and even if incidental speeches are vigorous. But these scenes, however derived, are put together by him and him alone. They may suit one another or not, as the gods determine. That is one reason why his comedies, however admirable in parts, are as wholes so ramshackle and haphazard, as if a man built a house with excellent rooms but no staircases. The other chief reason is that he allows an effective scene to tail off into incongruous buffoonery, as if in the house just described we came upon people cooking in the library or playing bridge in the bathroom.

It is a confirmation of this, that whatever feats of clever construction we do find occur in the body of a scene. The *Mostellaria* has an excellent sleight to make a breakdown in the plot help the plot. Tranio, to conceal the dissipation of his young master on the sudden return of the old master Theopropides, bundles the revellers inside the house with a command to make no sound. When the father arrives, Tranio keeps him from entering his own house by a story that it is haunted by the ghost of a murdered man, wherefore the young master has gone, and it is deserted. Just as Theopropides is growing impressed, one of the concealed revellers shouts from within " Hi! Tranio! " (515). The old man pricks up his ears, but Tranio feverishly pretends that this is the ghost's voice and so induces Theopropides to flee in terror. That is admirable, but it does not join the interview to any later scene.

Much less discussion is demanded here by the third and fourth chief elements in dramatic structure — the *peripeteia* and the solution that it provides. His *peripeteia* is as a rule not strictly a " recoil " at all, but a mechanically intrusive event, a mere accident invaluable both to the characters and to the playwright, but not arising naturally out of the antecedent action. It corresponds to what is termed in tragedy " the god from the machine." Such a god is actually found in *Amphitruo*, and there his intervention is entirely justified, since a god is among the *dramatis personae* from the beginning and has always intended to set everything right. This, therefore, is one of the very few places in all dramatic literature where (owing to the nature of the story) the god from the machine is an entirely legitimate device.[63]

But that play is unique among his extant works, being (as the prologue remarks) a tragi-comedy. The *Mercator,* too, stands apart, as we have shown at some length; its *peripeteia* is excellent. As for the other eighteen plays, some have no genuine *peripeteia* at all — *Aulularia, Casina, Cistellaria, Mostellaria, Stichus,* and *Truculentus;* some contain a *peripeteia* that is a mere accidental intrusion into the plot — *Captivi, Curculio, Epidicus, Rudens,* and *Trinummus;* the rest have a climax indeed that brings about the solution, but it is the natural and expected outcome of a plan devised by some of the characters — *Asinaria, Bacchides, Menaechmi, Miles, Persa, Poenulus,* and *Pseudolus.* As for this last class, it may be held that such plays are none the worse for such a climax, and that if they fail to show a *peripeteia* as we have defined it, then so much the worse for our definition. But it cannot be denied that the greatest dramatic thrill is felt when a conscious plot produces a result entirely different, or at least divergent, from that intended by the plotters. For instance, the solution of the *Miles* is less attractive than that of the *Mercator:* in plays like the latter we have the peculiar pleasure of amused surprise entirely divorced from disbelief; whereas in the *Miles*-type we know exactly what is to come,

[ 97 ]

and though it is pleasant to see Pyrgopolinices duped into actually sending away the heroine with her lover, we have no thrill of discovery. Most of the *peripeteiae* are vastly less good, in particular those of the second class, where all is put right by a sudden discovery, as that the heroine is an Athenian's daughter. The works in our first class, having no *peripeteia*, are not really plays at all. If the reader is inclined to regard this as absurd pedantry, let him disregard our phrases and consider those writings in themselves. He will find, as we have freely confessed, excellent scenes in some of the six; but what does he think of the *Mostellaria* as a whole, where the grievous and long-continued offence of Philolaches is at the last moment freely and casually condoned by his father merely because his drunken companion wakes up in time to request that this should be done? What of *Stichus*, which falls into three mere lumps? The *Aulularia* is much better than these, but a character-sketch is not a play: we demand the balance and poise of a rational structure in the whole action. That these faulty or feeble climaxes (like the flaws and stupidities in development-scenes) are due to *contaminatio*, forms no rebuttal of the charge that Plautus constructs badly. If he is to be called a dramatist, he should use his materials, however derived, with some attention to rational organization.

From all our discussions it becomes evident that Plautus' quality cannot be summed in one statement. It would be foolish to strike an average between — let us say — *Two Gentlemen of Verona* and *Macbeth* with the result that Shakespeare was placed rather high in the second class. There is no less disparity between the *Mercator* and *Stichus*. When Plautus is nothing but a translator, the outcome is a thoroughly first-rate light comedy; when he translates with a considerable admixture of his own work, we find an attractive but deplorably patchy affair, part good Attic work, part good or bad Atellane; when he gives himself a very free hand, the result is merely abject. Plautus is a master of Latin; he has a strong sense of boisterous hearty fun; as an original playwright he does not exist.

# V. TERENCE: INTRODUCTION

**P**UBLIUS TERENTIUS AFER was born at Carthage about the date of Plautus' death, probably in 185 B.C., possibly as much as ten years earlier, and died in 159. He was a native of Africa (as his cognomen proves) and apparently a mulatto or a quadroon: Suetonius'[64] description says *mediocri statura, gracili corpore, colore fusco* — " of middling stature, slender and swarthy." In childhood he was brought to Rome and became the slave of one Terentius Lucanus, who, moved by his talent and bodily grace, gave him an excellent education in both Latin and Greek, later bestowing on him freedom and his own name. Terence early became a friend and protégé of the illustrious Scipio Africanus Minor and the brilliant group of young Hellenizing nobles that surrounded him. Perhaps by their liberality he acquired a small estate; his daughter married a Roman knight. Terence produced six comedies:[65] *Andria* (" The Girl of Andros " — an island near the coast of

Attica), based on the *Andria* and *Perinthia* of
Menander, in 166; *Hecyra* (" The Mother-in-
law "), based on the *Hecyra* of Apollodorus,
in 165, again in 160, and (a revised version) in
the same year; *Heautontimorumenos* (" Self-
Punishment "), based on Menander's work of
the same title, in 163; *Eunuchus* (" The Eunuch "), in 161, based on Menander's work
of the same title, with additions from his *Colax*
(" Flatterer "); *Phormio* (name of the princi-
pal character), based on Apollodorus' *Epidicazomenos* [66] (" The Litigant "), in 161; *Adelphoe* (" The Brothers ") also in 161, based on
Menander's work of the same title, with an
insertion, according to the prologue, of a scene
from the *Synapothnescontes* (" Dying Together ") of Diphilus. He then journeyed to
Greece and Asia Minor, wishing to study and
to collect plays of Menander, but died on the
way home at the age of twenty-six or little
more. Some attributed his death to grief because certain new comedies that he had written were lost at sea.

The reputation of Terence, though at times
overshadowed, has never failed from his own
lifetime down to our own day. His prologues
contain tart replies to the strictures of the

" old poet " Luscius Lanuvinus, defending the practice of *contaminatio* which had fallen into disfavour with the generation of Caecilius, the distinguished comic dramatist whose date falls between those of Plautus and Terence. But with Caecilius himself our poet's relations appear to have been cordial. Suetonius relates an attractive story. When Terence, as an obscure youth of perhaps only eighteen years, offered his *Andria* to the aedile in charge of the Megalesian festival, the magistrate sent him to submit his work to Caecilius. The great man was at dinner and, unimpressed by his shabbily-dressed visitor, bade him sit on a stool beside the dining-couch and read his manuscript. After a few lines, Caecilius stopped him, made him join his repast, and later listened to the rest of the play with lively admiration. In public his success was more dubious. The *Hecyra* was heard to the end only at its third production: the first attempt was ruined by the hostility of the audience, the second by the report of a gladiator-show.[67] But the *Eunuch* pleased so much that it was immediately given again and earned for its author a greater sum than had ever been received for a comedy — 8000 sesterces. A few

years after his death all the plays, except
*Hecyra* and *Adelphoe,* had been revived.[68]
We have some striking comments from individuals. The distinguished dramatist Afranius
wrote: " Will you compare anyone with Terence? " — *Terenti num similem dicetis quem-
piam?* Volcacius Sedigitus placed him only
sixth in his canon of ten comic playwrights.[69]
Julius Caesar wrote some notable verses which
we shall discuss later. Cicero in a few juvenile
and enthusiastic lines [70] praises Terence for
his choice style (*lectus sermo*), quietness (*se-
dati motus*), urbanity and charm of utterance.
Varro awarded him the palm for characterization, and sets him up as the model of *mediocri-
tas,* the style " intermediate " between the richness (*ubertas*) of Pacuvius and the spareness
(*gracilitas*) of Lucilius.[71] Horace reports [72]
the opinion that while Caecilius is eminent for
dignity (*gravitas*) Terence is eminent for
" art " — whatever may be the precise meaning of *ars* here. Horace himself was clearly
akin to Terence in temperament, and imitates
him occasionally. Quintilian, despite his dole-
ful view of Roman Comedy, at least allows
these works " the height of elegance." [73] In
antiquity a long series of scholars gave atten-

tion to these comedies; we still possess, for all save *Heautontimorumenos*, the invaluable commentary of Donatus, though by no means in its original state. The repute of Terence stood very high in the Middle Ages. German literature is said to begin with Hroswitha, the learned nun of Gandersheim who in the tenth century, desirous of weaning the faithful from their love of pagan Terence, composed six little Latin plays in supposed imitation of his manner but extremely edifying in matter. It was on the least bad of these, *Paphnutius*, that Anatole France based his *Thais*. In England Terence was long the text-book for beginners in Latin, and many of our plays are imitated from his, whether directly or through Italian and French. Nevertheless, our most authentically Terentian stylist is not a dramatist at all, but a novelist — George Meredith.

Two controversial topics must next be faced. Gossip said that the Scipionic circle collaborated with him, and his prologues twice refer to this rumour with complacency, neither accepting nor contradicting it.[74] The importance of this help has been variously estimated: at one extreme is the belief that Terence was merely a mouthpiece of Hellenizing nobles who

did not wish to be known as writers for the
stage, precisely as some affirm that Shakespeare took responsibility for the writings of
Bacon or the Earl of Oxford; at the other is
the supposition that Scipio and the rest helped
Terence only by providing a congenial atmosphere — and in such "collaboration" everyone will believe. Granted the style of Terence
and his known friendship with this circle, such
a charge was certain in any case to be brought,
particularly by malicious rivals. Therefore its
existence proves nothing. Further, if these
comedies are the work of various hands, it is
surprising that we can detect no internal evidence of such co-operation — no unevenness
of style, no varieties of versification, no
wrenching of construction (unless indeed this
is to be detected in the Thraso-Gnatho scenes
of the *Eunuch*), above all, no scrap of satire
on contemporary Romans or allusions to
events of the day, such as Laelius, one imagines, would have inserted. It was indeed Laelius at whom report most definitely pointed.
Nepos [75] relates a story of delightful particularity. "On the first of March, one year,
Gaius Laelius was at his villa near Puteoli.
His wife reminded him that dinner was early,

but he begged not to be interrupted. Later he entered the dining-room behind time, saying that he had not often found writing go so well. Being asked to let them hear what he had written, he recited those verses in *Self-Punishment: satis pol proterve me Syri promissa huc induxerunt* etc." (723). One feels perverse enough to say that such evidence is too good. The most natural view is that Terence received nothing more than invaluable encouragement and sympathy from his powerful and cultivated friends, sometimes (no doubt) suggestions as to which Greek comedy he should select — just as Charles II recommended a Spanish play to John Crowne — and, it may be, advice as to treatment. A strong argument against such implications as those of Nepos is found in the second *Hecyra*-prologue,[76] where the veteran actor Ambivius Turpio is caused by the poet to relate how his encouragement kept Terence at work when almost driven by his enemies to renounce his art for good. Finally, the reminder is not uncalled for, that even if Scipio or Laelius wrote every word of these comedies, they remain no worse and no better than they were. For the man Terence in himself we care little;

it is the plays that matter, enormously more than the means by which they came into being. Here and hereafter we shall take leave to say "Terence" when we mean the writer.

It is more important to observe that he wrote first for a clique and then courageously stepped forward from that sheltered position. The former statement is proved by the boldness, the acid superiority, of his rebukes to Luscius Lanuvinus and to the "stupid populace" itself; and to some degree by the brilliant intellectualism, the refusal of Plautine boisterousness, the silver Atticism that pervades his work. But he also makes it abundantly plain that he is not content to remain the laureate of an intelligentsia. He insists on taking his place in the national literature and would convert the populace to accepting and relishing a new type of comedy. "Be fair," he exclaims. "Give me a chance to grow. I give you a chance to see new and faultless plays":

> *facite aequi sitis: date crescendi copiam,*
> *novarum qui spectandi faciunt copiam*
> *sine vitiis.*[77]

In *The Mother-in-Law* he delivers a fine appeal:

> *vobis datur*
> *potestas condecorandi ludos scaenicos.*
> *nolite sinere per vos artem musicam*
> *recidere ad paucos.*

" With you lies the power to favour dramatic
shows. Do not suffer this art to fall into the
hands of a few." The last words may mean:
" Do not force drama into becoming the hobby
of a clique," but more probably they mean:
" Do not allow the old gang to keep young in-
novators out in the cold." The appeal failed.
It was about this time that the prologue to
the revived *Casina* sneered at the " new writers " as more worthless than the new coin-
age — *multo sunt nequiores quam nummi
novi.*[78] Whatever might have happened had
he lived, Terence died very young, and his
type of comedy soon followed him.

The other controversial topic is the originality of Terence — using that name (as we said)
for the person who wrote these six comedies.
Even if Laelius composed them all during holi-
days in his country-house, and the young Afri-
can was but a go-between, this problem is unchanged.

Each is based on a Greek play of the New
Comedy, sometimes with *contaminatio*. These

[ 108 ]

Greek works are all lost, save for a meagre collection of fragments. The question is: How much of Terence is nevertheless original? The words " based on " were used just now so as not to beg the question. Terence began always by considering a Greek comedy. What was his own completed work? There are five possibilities.

(i) His finished play was a mere translation, as close as verse-composition would allow, like Dr. A. S. Way's version of Euripides.

(ii) While entirely faithful to the original in details of structure and development, it was nevertheless coloured by the translator's temperament, interests and knowledge, like Professor Gilbert Murray's versions of the same poet.

(iii) While following the original as in (ii) it inserted new scenes or even new characters, as does Dryden's *Amphitryon*.

(iv) Taking the story of the original in its details, it nevertheless changed the tone and import of the whole, as does Mr. Shaw's rendering of Herr Trebitsch's *Frau Gittas Sühne*.

(v) Using the original as a mere starting-point, it became a more or less independent play, as Shelley's *Prometheus* owns but an external connexion with the Aeschylean drama.

Of these, the first and fifth are certainly untenable: the commentary of Donatus makes it plain that Terence diverges from Menander and Apollodorus and also that his mere outline of events, at any rate, is very close to theirs. The second must be abandoned in favour of the third: Donatus tells us, for instance, that Antipho of the *Eunuchus* is not in Menander's play but was inserted by Terence. Of the remaining possibilities, the third is accepted by practically all scholars. The present writer, however, accepts the fourth. It cannot be too strongly emphasized that similarity in mere " story " does not necessarily make one play an imitation of, or even like, another. Two faces may be anatomically alike, while their expressions give them an utterly different appearance.

A complete discussion would be out of place here: we must mention briefly the most significant points. The current view has often been fully and eloquently put. We cannot translate Terence back into Greek iambics and trochaics of 300 B.C. and rejoice that we have discovered four new comedies of Menander and two of Apollodorus, not to mention a scene of Diphilus; but we can be sure that we have the gist of their work and — here is a notable point — may therefore use it as evidence for their dramaturgy, temperament and views. Thus Wilamowitz-Moellendorff writes: [79] " In the *Heautontimorumenos* Menander allows the passage of a night ": he is arguing, not from any Greek passage, but from the Terentian play. Legrand in his monumental *Daos* incessantly uses the Latin works as evidence for or against any detail of Greek comedy that he may be discussing. Impressive support for this view is to be found in ancient writers. Cicero, in the verses already mentioned, writes that Terence has " published Menander turned and rendered in Latin ":

*conversum expressumque Latina voce Menandrum in medium nobis sedatis motibus effers.*

Donatus' commentary now and again mentions divergences of phrasing between Terence and Menander,[80] which implies close agreement elsewhere. Above all, Terence himself talks in his prologue as if — except for *contaminatio* — he were a mere translator: the Diphilus-passage in the *Adelphoe*, he says, is " translated word for word " (*verbum de verbo expressum extulit*).[81] Surely these three evidences put the matter beyond dispute?

Nevertheless, this view cannot stand. We shall first set out arguments for our own theory and shall thereafter deal with the evidence of Terence, Donatus, and Cicero.

Terence takes over " the story," the mere external events, from Menander, just as Shakespeare took his from Plutarch or Bandello or English political history, and as Molière took his *Amphitryon* from Plautus. But the plot — the spiritual, moral, artistic development — is his own. In the course of this construction he at times took a passage, perhaps a whole scene, from the Greek because it suited his purpose, exactly as an Italian architect of the *cinquecento* used wrought blocks from Roman temples for a building that was artistically his own. The literary manner of Terence was undoubtedly learned from Menander: the similarity is amazing when we consider the difference between Latin and Greek as exemplified by Ennius and Euripides.[82] Nay, more: we should be foolish to deny that Terence learned much concerning dramatic method from his Greek forerunners,

as Ibsen trained himself on Sardou and Scribe.
But the six comedies we possess are, as examples of dramatic art, original. Of the arguments that support this view two shall be
stated here.

Julius Caesar, as we learn from Suetonius'
life of Terence, wrote thus:

> *tu quoque, tu in summis, O dimidiate Menander,*
> *poneris, et merito, puri sermonis amator.*
> *lenibus atque utinam scriptis adiuncta foret vis,*
> *comica ut aequato virtus polleret honore*
> *cum Graecis neve hac despectus parte iaceres!*
> *unum hoc maceror ac doleo tibi desse, Terenti.*

" You also, Half-Menander, are placed in the
front rank, and rightly, you lover of limpid
style. And would that force had been added
to your smooth writing, so that your excellence
in comedy might lord it in honour equal with
the Greeks, and you might not be whelmed in
disrepute on that side! Your lack of this one
merit is anguish and grief to me, Terence."
What is this force, power, energy, wherein Terence so lamentably falls below the Greeks? [83]
It is certain that no element of style is intended. Caesar has just praised Terence's literary manner; and if it is suggested [84] that

[ 113 ]

*vis* means majesty of style — contrasted with
the smoothness to which Caesar does refer —
the answer is: first, that such a view does
not suit the passage, for Caesar goes on to
talk of excellence in comedy, and to such excellence majesty is foreign; second, that whatever merits Menander possesses, we have no
reason at all to include majesty among them.
No: is not literary power; and that one fact
is immensely strong support for our theory.
For, whether the " force " resides in exposition of incidental topics, or in characterization,
or in plot-construction, or (most general of
all) in the selection of a theme for dramatic
composition, matters nothing at present. One,
or more than one, of these it must be: for,
leaving style on one side, there is nothing else
in any non-lyric play ever written since writing
began. Now, if Terence were merely a translator, these kinds of force could not possibly
disappear in his hands, and therefore Caesar
could not bewail their absence. The unmistakable inference is that Terence learned, indeed, his style from Menander, but went his
own way as a dramatist — a worse way, according to the critic; but his own.

Vastly more cogent — for Caesar's evidence

is that of but one reader — is a proof that rises from the whole body of Terentian drama. These six comedies, when examined in the order of their appearance, reveal a steady and marked advance in dramatic excellence.[85] This progress shall be demonstrated at large in later paragraphs; a few general remarks may be offered now. Assuming for the moment that this undeviating progress is proved, it instantly refutes the current idea that Terence is no more than a copyist. If he were, we should have to suppose that he began by translating weak plays and worked his way up to the best gradually. Such a notion is absurd; would any Swede open a series of Shakespearean versions with *Pericles* and proceed cautiously through *Cymbeline* and *Coriolanus* to *Macbeth?* But researches were so long devoted to anise and cummin, the *brevis brevians* and classification of adjectives, that serious study of these plays as plays was woefully neglected. Even now there exist scarcely any books that study the development of Terence as a playwright. Once he is so considered, this development and its implications will become evident.[86] A skilful demonstration [87] has indeed been offered that Terence shows no improvement in power so to mortise a passage into the main body that the joints escape the eye, or to deal dextrously with a pause that in the Greek original was devoted to a lyric interlude. But this proves only what will be cheerfully granted: that he is not perfect. He is launching out and making his own mistakes. This weakness in *contaminatio* and the rest may be proved, but it remains microscopic. We shall see that it is utterly overshadowed by an increasing vigour, scope, resourcefulness in construction, particularly by the development of a new and magnificent device.

But what of the three formidable witnesses on the other side — Cicero, Donatus, Terence himself? As for Cicero, everything he writes about both Plautus and Terence shows that he has no feeling at all for drama as drama, only for the wit, fun, brilliance of language that he detects and relishes. So frequent was this kind of " criticism " among Romans, that it is not in the least disingenuous to assert that Cicero's statement concerning translation of Menander is entirely compatible with the existence of many passages where Terence is not translating Menander at all. His words need mean no more than what everyone admits — that the Diphilus-scene (for example) is a genuine translation.

Donatus is more perplexing. At first sight his evidence might appear to contradict us flatly; but the more we examine his commentary the more doubtful we shall grow. Is it not strange that his general statement concerning Terence's indebtedness to Greek should be explicitly based on some other authority, not on his own? "Two *are said* to be translated from Apollodorus . . . the other four from Menander." Yet he must have had Menander at his elbow while writing his detailed and lengthy notes. Why this doubt? Moreover, in the course of those notes, though (as we have agreed) he constantly implies indebtedness, he also constantly implies originality. We are not now referring to those divergent phrases already mentioned, but to other places where we find tacit implication, which is all the more impressive. Only one specimen shall be given. On *Hecyra* 774 he writes: " Terence, relying on his art, has made many bold strokes, creating (*facit*) kind mothers-in-law and honourable courtesans in defiance of tradition. But so warily does he supply motives based on reason and antecedent facts, that we feel that he, and he alone, has a right to perfect freedom." It is known that our text of Donatus contains later additions. This may help to account in some degree for our difficulty. But "Donatus" as he stands is an extremely dubious witness to the current doctrine that these plays are mere versions.

The statements of Terence himself need cause less perplexity. His prologues are deeply interesting, but they are highly disingenuous. We have seen how he evades the report that Scipio and his friends constantly collaborated with him. So of his debt to Greece. At one time he implies that he is the whole-hearted translator; at another he calls his plays novelties. He claims the support of the public against the "old gang" who insist that dramas should not be "contaminated." He would have it both ways: he is following the stream and he has his back to the wall. Again, the third and last edition of the *Hecyra* is called "entirely new" (*plane est pro nova*).[88] Therefore, if this or its predecessor was a genuine translation, either its predecessor or this must be something other than a genuine translation. Of *Self-Punishment* he tells us that he has taken the Menandrian work, but from a simple plot has evolved a double plot. Let anyone look at the play and imagine it with one of the love-affairs deleted! As Terence has written it, the play depends entirely on their interlocking. In short, we must not accept his statements without supporting evidence. He is a young foreigner, seeking to establish himself on the stage in face of fierce and continuous opposition from older writers; therefore he seeks to gain whatever credit may be due to a loyal translator of the Greek models, and also whatever credit there is in dashing enterprise.

Borrowings, improvements, degradations have so long and so often been the chief theme of Terentian scholars that we are startled, not only delighted, to realize that all the time these plays themselves have been awaiting us, unchanged and smiling. If we can admire a birch-forest in spring without a preliminary lecture on the geology of the district, if we are content to appreciate a beautiful woman even before we learn from which parent she inherits her looks, then we may read and enjoy these six comedies with small misgiving. " Enjoy " is, indeed, the best word. There are Latin

writers who surpass Terence in greatness,
beauty, their power to illuminate: he stands on
the level of Horace and Livy, not of Virgil and
Tacitus. But for sheer enjoyment, the quiet
enduring relish we feel for that specially beloved band, the artists who seem to transcend
ourselves not infinitely, Terence is unsur-
passed. In spirit he belongs to eighteenth-
century France and England, not to Rome of
the Punic Wars.

Let us endeavour to describe his excellence,
passing from the less to the more dramatic
qualities.

# VI. TERENCE: STYLE:
## MORALIZING

FIRST, then, for his style. His native
language was some Libyan *patois;*
Latin he acquired in boyhood and
Greek while yet a stripling. These studies,
acting upon an alert and sensitive mind, made
his Latin a speech that in limpidity and ease
far surpasses that of his predecessors, his con-
temporaries, and, indeed, most of his successors. Again and again we are reminded of
Synge's English and Heine's German. The
feel of his style is like satin. "Terence shares
with his master the praise of an amenity that
is like Elysian speech, equable and ever gracious; like the face of the Andrian's young
sister: *adeo modesto, adeo venusto, ut nihil
supra.*" [89] This "perfection of chaste loveli-
ness" can be admired equally in all the plays:
here, it is gladly confessed, he makes no advance. It is hard to see where improvement
is possible in this urbanity, this crystalline
charm. Take a simple instance (*Phormio*
91 ff.):

*interea dum sedemus illi, intervenit*
*adulescens quidam lacrumans. nos mirarier;*
*rogamus quid sit. 'numquam aeque' inquit 'ac*
   *modo*
*paupertas mihi onus visumst et miserum et grave.*
*modo quandam vidi virginem viciniae*
*miseram suam matrem lamentari mortuam.*
*ea sita erat exadvorsum neque illi benivolens*
*neque notus neque cognatus extra unam aniculam*
*quisquam aderat qui adiutaret funus: miseritumst.'*

English must blur this, apparently. " As we
sat there, in comes a certain youth, weeping.
In wonder we asked what ailed him. 'Never
till now,' he says, 'did I understand what a
grievous heavy load is poverty. Just now I
saw an unhappy girl who lives hard by, mourn-
ing for her dead mother. She sat facing the
body: with her there was no one to aid her in
the funeral but one old woman — no friend,
no acquaintance, no relative. I pitied her.' "

This nimbleness and clarity have produced
celebrated epigrams or proverbial phrases:

*hinc illae lacrimae (Andria* 126)
" hence these tears."

*amantium irae amoris integratiost (Ib.* 555)
" lovers' quarrels are the strengthening of love "
     (" the falling-out that all the more endears ").

[ 122 ]

*homo sum: humani nil a me alienum puto* (*Heaut.* 77)
" I am a man: anything that touches man is my business."

*nullumst iam dictum quod non sit dictum prius* (*Eun.* 41)
" there is no saying of our day that has not been said before."

(It was while lecturing on this passage, to a class containing the future St. Jerome, that Donatus burst out into the even more famous words, *pereant qui ante nos nostra dixerunt!* — " Curse the people who anticipate our epigrams! ")

*nihilo plus agas quam si des operam ut cum ratione insanias* (*Ib.* 62 f.)
" You might just as well endeavour to be mad sensibly " (or " on a system ").

*fortes fortuna adiuvat* (*Phormio* 203)
" Fortune favours the brave."

*quot homines tot sententiae* (*Ib.* 454)
" As many opinions as people."

*erubuit: salva res est* (Ad. 643)
" All's well: he blushes."

[ 123 ]

Less familiar but equally admirable phrases could be quoted in abundance: *ut homost, ita morem geras* (*Ad.* 431) — "humour a man as he is" ("You can preach to mites only in terms of cheese"); *hoc ubi fit, ibi non vere vivitur* (*Heaut.* 154) [90] — "where that happens, life is based on shams"; *quantist sapere! numquam accedo quin abs te abeam doctior* (*Eun.* 791) — "How priceless is wit! I never come near you without walking away the wiser man."

Downright jokes are far less frequent in Terence than in Plautus, because the former writes high comedy, the latter usually broad comedy or farce; and high comedy might theoretically — in practice, this is naturally not so — contain not a single joke. Unlike the French, we have constantly to remind ourselves that comedy is not necessarily an affair of jokes at all. The Terentian type, found earlier in *Arbitration* and later in *Tartuffe*, arouses and appeals to our intellectual sense of human follies. "The test of true Comedy," writes Meredith,[91] "is that it shall awaken thoughtful laughter"; and further:

" If you believe that our civilization is founded
in common-sense (and it is the first condition of
sanity to believe it), you will, when contemplating
men, discern a Spirit overhead; not more heavenly
than the light flashed upward from glassy surfaces,
but luminous and watchful; so closely attached to
them that it may be taken for a slavish reflex, until
its features are studied. It has the sage's brows,
and the sunny malice of a faun lurks at the corners
of the half-closed lips drawn in an idle wariness of
half tension. That slim feasting smile, shaped like
the long-bow, was once a big round satyr's laugh,
that flung up the brows like a fortress lifted by
gunpowder. The laugh will come again, but it will
be of the order of the smile, finely tempered, show-
ing sunlight of the mind, mental richness rather
than noisy enormity."

That elegance which we noted in narrative
and isolated phrases appears in the texture of
Terentian dialogue. His people never wander
from the point into buffoonery, or even fun,
that is irrelevant; rarely even into brilliant
chat unwarranted by the plot, like Onesimus'
theological sermon at the close of Menander's
*Arbitration*. Urbanity, crispness, an amiable
yet steady insistence on the business in hand,
pervade these works. Instances are of course

not easy to give, as the effect is perceived by
perusal of a considerable passage. But observe
the nimbleness of this (*Phormio* 109 ff.):

GETA.  *ille qui illam amabat fidicinam tantum modo*
       *' satis' inquit ' scitast '; noster vero —*
DAV.                              *iam scio:*
       *amare coepit.*
GETA.                *scin quam? quo evadat vide.*

" The youth who (as I told you) is in love
with the music-girl merely said ' Rather
pretty '; but our young gentleman — " " I
know: he fell in love with her." " Ah, but
how? Hear the result." Longer instances
may be found in plenty: the conversation between Syra and Parmeno (*Hecyra* 63 ff.), the
beautiful final talk of Pamphilus and Bacchis
(*Hecyra* 855 ff.), and the renowned narrative of Simo that opens the *Andria*.

An attractive result of thus keeping to the
point is that although Terence often moralizes,
such passages are never tedious. His admirable miniature sermons are never dragged in,
but always arise clearly from the situation.
They are not to be found in the *Andria,* but
begin in *Self-Punishment,* where we find a passage (151 ff.) so germane to the business of

the play that it is hardly to be distinguished
from the ordinary dialogue:

*ingenio te esse in liberos leni puto*
*et illum obsequentem si quis recte aut commode*
*tractaret. verum nec tu illum satis noveras*
*nec te ille; hoc ubi fit, ibi non vere vivitur.*
*tu illum numquam ostendisti quanti penderes*
*nec tibi illest credere ausus quae est aequom patri.*
*quod si esset factum, haec numquam evenissent tibi.*

" You showed yourself gentle towards your
children, I believe; and your son was dutiful,
if he had been handled wisely or understand-
ingly. But you did not really know one another; where that happens, life is a sham.
You never let him see your fondness, nor did
he venture to give you the confidence a father
should receive. If he had, this would never
have happened to you." Later (502 ff.) Menedemus utters a brief soliloquy interesting for
two reasons. " Good heavens, how amazingly
human nature is made up! Everyone sees and
judges another's situation better than his own.
Is it because we are hampered in our own affairs by excessive joy or grief? How much
more sense Chremes shows on my behalf than
I show myself! " Chapman, the Elizabethan

[ 127 ]

dramatist, based his *All Fools* on this play, and his most striking passage reproduces this soliloquy:

> O *the good God of Gods,*
> *How blind is pride! What eagles we are still*
> *In matters that belong to other men,*
> *What beetles in our own!*

This insistence upon the keener sight of others indicates how deeply Terence was impressed by our helplessness if we stand alone: it is this conviction, as we shall see, that has led him to devise the most original element in his dramatic technique. In later plays the "morality" continues. The *Eunuch* contains a passage that remained in Shakespeare's mind from schooldays until he wrote *Hamlet*.[92] Horace, who not only resembles Terence but also borrows from him, has paraphrased it.[93] Parmeno reads his love-lorn master a sermon (57 ff.):

> *quae res in se neque consilium neque modum*
> *habet ullum, eam consilio regere non potes.*
> *in amore haec omnia insunt vitia: iniuriae,*
> *suspiciones, inimicitiae, indutiae,*
> *bellum, pax rursum: incerta haec si tu postules*
> *ratione certa facere, nihilo plus agas*
> *quam si des operam ut cum ratione insanias.*

"A thing that is without plan or system it is impossible to govern by system. In love are all these faults: wrongs, suspicions, quarrels, reconciliations, war, then peace. If you expect to carry on these shifting relations by a fixed method, you will find no more success than if you try to use method in madness." *Phormio* contains some excellent thoughts (241 ff.) on fortifying the heart against sorrow. Sostrata's beautiful speech (*Hecyra* 593 ff.) to her son is so wonderfully conceived that we cannot say it is moralizing at all rather than a strictly relevant description of the causes of her action. The same is true of Micio's wise admonition to Demea (*Adelphoe* 820 ff.). We may remark in passing that it provides an admirable summary of Ibsen's main thought about ethics: that, no doubt, is why Donatus, who lived fifteen centuries before Ibsen, calls it "most obscure in matter and diction." It runs thus: [94]

"Have patience: I understand you; I was coming to that. There are many signs in men, brother, from which it is easy to conjecture, that when two persons do the same thing, one would be justified in saying, it may prove very hurtful to the one, but not so to the other, from no difference in the thing

[ 129 ]

itself, but in the persons who do it. I see in your sons what makes me confident they will answer our wishes. They have good sense, discretion, modesty enough upon occasion, and love one another entirely; whence 'tis easy to discern in them a noble nature and soul; you may at any time reclaim them."

Just the same complete fusion of moralizing with close comment on the situation appears in Demea's soliloquy (855 ff.) about the treatment that he and Micio have applied to the two youths. We find then under this head that development which we shall observe in more strictly dramatic qualities.

# VII. CHARACTERIZATION IN TERENCE

IN SOME types of drama the playwright's task here is plain enough, however difficult: he wishes us to believe in some man or woman as really existing. In this sense, Shakespeare when he created Hamlet and Marlowe when he created Tamburlaine were both doing exactly the same thing, however their creations differ in merit. But turn to the Comedy of Manners. There the dramatist wishes us to recognize everyday life on his stage and (in particular) to accept his persons as types, examples of which we have met often in the flesh. It would seem to follow that the hero of social comedy should combine features present in many individuals but should not exhibit special features possessed by few or none of his flesh-and-blood constituents: he should be an ethical description on two legs. Dramatic interest would then centre not, as in *Hamlet* and *Tamburlaine,* upon the doings and fate of one person, but upon the commerce of human beings in general, the value and effects of the prejudices, passions, *modus vivendi,* of a whole society. The playwright's task will not be vivid projection of character, but invention of revealing situations and dialogue. This, we have said, is what would seem to follow; and very often it does. Ben Jonson's comedies provide the best examples; one of them is actually named *Every Man in his Humour:* that is, here we are to find each person a vehicle and exponent of some "humour" — some ethical type. This is uniformly true of Jonson's work. Apply the test we mentioned earlier: [95] we cannot easily imagine his people in other situations than those described by the author. Volpone is shrewd cynicism in bed, testing a theory — excellently done; but can we imagine him at a card-party, or making love?

Meredith has written [96] that "the comic of Jonson is a scholar's excogitation of the comic"; say, rather, the pedant's: for this kind of drama is based, not on learning but on a notion that art can be produced by rules. Rules enable us to appreciate art (whatever chaotic "criticism" may allege); they can never produce it, their great but only value to the artist being to prevent blunders. Certainly one need not be a scholar to follow the Jonsonian method. It has been followed, with whatever varieties of lightness in treatment, of brilliance in dialogue, of excitement in the situations, by a host of writers: to mention only eminent English names, by Etherege, Wycherley, Congreve, Crowne, and Otway in Restoration days and those immediately subsequent, by Goldsmith and Sheridan later, in the nineteenth century by Wilde.

Nevertheless, a few admirable artists have transcended what seem the necessary limitations of social comedy. With amazing delicacy and adroitness they have bestowed genuine life, some tinge of individuality, upon what should, by hypothesis, be a composite portrait. Chief in this small number of playwrights stands Molière. His people are often the ordinary typical figures. But Tartuffe, Jourdain, Célimène are triumphantly successful creations of the sort we have now in mind. The hypocrite, the parvenu, and the coquette are all to be recognized here, precisely as in the Jonsonian dramaturgy and precisely as not in the Shakespearean. For all that, they are quickened into an authentic particular life as well as a general existence. Each is the common

type raised to a higher power, *homo sapiens*
with a genuine name and address, a nose of his
own and a voice that we do not confuse with
his neighbour's. Among the Greeks, Menander belongs to this class: he is, so far as his
fragments allow us to judge, certainly not
Molière's equal; but, as certainly, he too prac-
tises this delicate art of the individualized
type. With them stands Terence. Perhaps
six of his characters attain the excellence that
we have described; and under this head again
is observed that progression which we noted
as the strongest proof of his originality. For
there are no such characters in the *Andria* or
*Self-Punishment*. The *Eunuch* contains but
one, Thais the courtesan; and charming as she
is, of this particular skill she is no very striking
instance. In *Phormio* there are two, Chremes
and Phormio himself, both on a level with
Thais. The last two plays show a clear advance: Sostrata and Bacchis in the *Hecyra*,
Demea and Micio in the *Adelphoe*, are superb
examples of what may be termed the Molièr-
esque manner: the wise-hearted mother, the
good-natured courtesan, the crusty father, the
jolly bachelor uncle — all capitally drawn,
" just the type," but a great deal more than

the type. Let us look more closely at two of them.

Since the *Hecyra* is a study in married life, Sostrata, Philumena's mother-in-law, stands in the foreground and names the play. Her structural value is equalled by her excellence as a character-study — a marvel of tender serene strength, dignity that is never pride, patience that is never weakness, sympathy always wise and foresighted. At her first entrance she wins us by her reply (206 ff.) to Laches' reproaches: "Why you accuse me I know not — so may the gods love me and so may it be granted us to pass our lives together!" So far Terence gives us the type: now comes the touch of individuality (235 ff.). "But, my dear, suppose her reason for pretending to hate me is that she wishes to see more of her own mother?" This affectionate understanding, which shines out more clearly when she is alone (274 ff.), brings Sostrata forth at the sound of Philumena's distress, although she has been once already repulsed. Her last scene, where she announces to her son that she is determined to withdraw to the country house, is her greatest moment. Pamphilus has protested against her resigning

friends and social pleasures for his sake. Her
reply (593 ff.) is full, not of mere resignation,
but of quiet wisdom and kindness, with touches
(once more) of the individual woman:

> nil iam mihi istae res voluptatis ferunt:
> dum aetatis tempus tulit, perfuncta satis sum:
>   satias iam tenet
> studiorum istorum. haec mihi nunc curast maxuma,
>   ut ne quoi mea
> longinquitas aetatis obstet mortemve expectet meam.
> hic video me esse invisam inmerito: tempust me
>   concedere.
> sic optume, ut ego opinor, omnis causas praecidam
>   omnibus:
> et me hac suspicione exsolvam et illis morem gessero.
> sine me obsecro hoc ecfugere, volgus quod male
>   audit mulierum.

"They no longer give me any pleasure. I had
a full enjoyment of them while my years per-
mitted, but now I am tired of such pursuits.
My chief care now is that no one should look
forward to my death and chafe at my long-
drawn-out years. Here I find undeserved dis-
like: it is time for me to make way: that is the
best means I can see to deprive everyone of
all grievances. I shall free myself from this
suspicion and show them a kindness. Do allow

me to escape the accusation levelled against the mass of women." Comment must blur this; but in our quest for individuality let us note the gentle remonstrance against Philumena, the firmness of *praecidam,* and the hint that it is a charge of vulgar jealousy by which Sostrata is nerved to this vigour. Throughout the play, she wins the reward of all nobly selfless spirits, that the people among whom she moves reflect something of her radiance. Parmeno is restrained (327 ff.) from prying into Philumena's secret by the thought that he may thus compromise Sostrata. Pamphilus, in the midst of his longing for Philumena, puts his mother at the same height in his affection (601 f.). Laches, who begins by jeering, can at last, when he has listened to her words of withdrawal, utter language (620 ff.) not unfit to be set beside them.

Micio is Terence's best-drawn male character. He and his brother Demea hold opposed theories of education: Terence solves the dispute by a compromise between the systems, but during most of the action Micio is a far more "sympathetic" character than Demea. This being so, it would have been easy to make him a vulgar leering old wretch like

Demaenetus in Plautus or Otway's Sir Jolly
Jumble. Terence has portrayed a dignified
gentleman, indulgent to his " son " by reason
of a sincerely held and deliberately followed
conception of a father's duty. This dignity be-
tokens an honourable spirit. When he learns
that Aeschinus has seduced Pamphila, he feels,
speaks, and acts precisely as Demea or any
other severe moralist could wish. There is no
trace of loose archness here (592 f.):

*ego in hac re nil reperio, quam ob rem lauder tanto
    opere, Hegio:*
*meum officium facio: quod peccatum a nobis
    ortumst corrigo.*

" For my part, Hegio, I see in this affair no
reason why you should praise me so warmly.
I am doing my duty — setting right an offence
committed by us." Throughout, Micio shows
a consummate knowledge of life: his first soliloquy contains a witty example (28 ff.) — " it
is better to suffer what your wife fears has
happened to you, than what your parents
fear." A more impressive instance is the
shrewd admonition (820 ff.) he offers to Demea, who is exasperated by the discovery that,
after all his care, Ctesipho has been corrupted

no less than Aeschinus. It begins with that
Ibsenist passage quoted earlier, and goes on:

> at enim metuas ne ab re sint tamen
> omissiores paulo. o noster Demea,
> ad omnia alia aetate sapimus rectius;
> solum unum hoc vitium adfert senectus hominibus:
> adtentiores sumus ad rem omnes quam sat est:
> quod illos sat aetas acuet.

"But you fear they are somewhat too casual
about money. Ah, my dear Demea, we grow
in wisdom, as in years, concerning all things
else, but age brings men this one fault: we are
all too set upon money. Time will sharpen
them as to that." Such a man is able to face
facts. Despite his theory of education, he confesses to us (141 ff.) his anxiety about Aeschinus' wildness, and later (737 ff.) to Demea
himself; above all, his good heart and knowledge of life appear magnificently in the explanation between him and his " son." The
old man comes suddenly upon the younger as
he falters beside Sostrata's door, brings him
to the point by telling of an alleged rival from
Miletus, and leads him on to vigorous but absurd opposition to this imaginary wedding. At
last Aeschinus bursts into tears and begins to

confess, whereupon Micio calms his fears, but firmly rebukes him for his terrible lack of courage and decision. All ends well: "Cheer up! you shall marry her" (626). As for individual traits, they are notable throughout, and especially in the later scenes where Demea beats Micio at his own game. That is, Micio adds to the excellently drawn character-type an admirable wit and a strong sense of fun. Even in that beautiful scene with Aeschinus, he can banter the youth. Aeschinus exclaims that he loves his "father" above all. Micio asks: "What! more than the lady?" (702). This is natural and pleasant, but it shows him stepping from his lofty place as a rebuker of criminal weakness: it prepares us for later passages, where Demea's frenzied wrath about Ctesipho is answered with ludicrous ribaldry. We may think it in bad taste — it assuredly would be so now — or welcome it as light relief to an extremely unfarcical play. The point to seize is that these things individualize him. He is not merely the traditional *lepidus senex* — "the jolly old man": he is Micio.

# VIII. PLOT–STRUCTURE IN TERENCE

STRESS has been laid on a steady improvement that can be watched through these six comedies when studied in chronological order. We are now to observe it in the most fundamental part of a playwright's work, structure. From first to last Terence devotes great attention to plot, but does not at first succeed: in fact we cannot regard him as a master of construction till *Phormio*. In the two latest plays he employs the perfected method with still greater ease, boldness and versatility.

The *Andria* shows grave faults amid undoubted merits. Simo's change of purpose provides a delightful entanglement. Having urged his son's acceptance of a marriage that Simo himself does not really wish, he is so pleased by Pamphilus' feigned eagerness that he decides to turn the sham into earnest. As he expounds this change of plan to Davus, Pamphilus' valet, we can imagine the slave's jaw

dropping as he realizes that Pamphilus' pretended acceptance (devised by Davus) has
been too convincing. Still more sophisticated
comedy is found in the scene of the midwife.
The stage-convention, it will be remembered,
was that all business, however domestic or indeed secret, should be transacted in the street
or at the doorway. Terence naturally chafed
at such nonsense, and here he hits back beautifully. After Glycerium's baby is born, the
midwife comes out and, as usual, bawls her
instructions from the door-step — " give her
a bath at once " etc. (483 ff.). Simo has already begun to overreach himself with a too
cunning idea that Glycerium's confinement is
a figment of Davus. The midwife's action con-
firms it. " Instead of telling them in the bed-
room what the patient needed, she waited till
she got outside and shouted from the pave-
ment to the women inside! Oh, Davus! Do
you despise me as much as that? Do you
think me a proper dupe for such obvious plots?
You might have taken some pains about it,
so that, if I found out, I might think you had
at any rate some fear of me " (490 ff.). This
is wit indeed. Simo's reproach, uttered less in
anger at the supposed conspiracy than in grief

at its badness, gives help to the construction;
and in the same moment it utters trenchant
satire on a stupid stage-convention. Terence
has used his very limitations: a method which
seems to ruin dramatic art is turned into a
novel and effective means of construction.

But the flaws are much greater. Little need
be said about Sosia, the " protatic " character.
Such people, as we have seen, were never ex-
pelled from the theatre: Terence himself uses
them in later plays,[97] and they flourish even
today. There are far more serious things.
We gradually realize that the contriving slave
himself makes no real contribution to the plot.
Of course Davus provides much incidental excitement and fun, but what does he perform?
In reality he is but a fifth wheel on the coach.
He produces a device that looks formidably
knowing and subtle, that Pamphilus should
pretend compliance with Simo's plan of a marriage with Philumena. But what is the outcome of this masterpiece? Firstly, Byrria's
discovery, which leads nowhere (see the next
paragraph). Further, Simo's sudden idea of
turning the sham marriage into earnest; but
that too comes to nothing at last. As for
Davus' elaborate orchestration of Chremes,

Mysis, and the baby, it is impossible — at any rate for one reader — to explain the deliberate bungling that he introduces. Nor does he in any way help to bring about the *peripeteia,* Crito's arrival, which involves the recognition of Glycerium as Chremes' daughter and therefore a possible wife for Pamphilus.

Further, Charinus (the second lover) and his man Byrria are structurally useless. They look important, to be sure: Charinus wishes to marry Philumena, and Byrria abets him. But the two love-interests do not genuinely affect one another in action. When Byrria discovers that Pamphilus, after assuring Charinus that he does not wish to marry Philumena, tells Simo (untruthfully) that he does, this supposed discovery of Pamphilus' deception of Charinus ought to produce counter-plots of Charinus that shall affect the Pamphilus-Glycerium affair. But no: hearing Byrria's news, Charinus — quite sensibly, of course — straightway confronts Pamphilus and is at once told the facts. Byrria's discovery could be deleted without loss, and a little further thought will show that the rest of the Charinus-Byrria part could follow it.

But could it? Here, if anywhere in the

study of Roman drama — nay, of drama in general — it is worth while to attempt the extreme of caution and particularity. Careful study, or rather balanced thinking, here will show us just how Terence worked. These Charinus-scenes have been proved structurally useless to the "question of the play" — what is to become of the Pamphilus-Glycerium affair in face of Simo's determination that Pamphilus shall marry Philumena? On this side, then, the play is bad. But, as often, the bungle reveals the writer's purpose far better than would success. For *ars est celare artem:* conversely, an artistic breakdown exhibits the artist's method. So does it come about that the adventure of peering over a poet's shoulder is here more delightful than at any other moment of Terence's career.

These scenes are useless. Then why does the playwright put them in? "Put in" is exactly correct: Terence has obtruded them upon his "original," the *Andria* of Menander. Donatus writes on v. 301: "These characters are not in Menander: Terence has added them to the play . . ." Why? Few assumptions are less dangerous than that Menander's plot was soundly constructed. Therefore, if Ter-

[ 145 ]

ence takes the initiative so drastically, it is certain that to him the intended matter must have seemed in some way vital. Donatus tells us his idea of the reason: "Terence has added them to the play lest it should be too painful to leave Philumena scorned or unbetrothed while Pamphilus marries another." This is excellent, so far as it goes. But does it meet the objections we have raised against the Charinus-scenes? Yes and no. The "question of the play," we have just said, is Pamphilus' trouble; the climax, or *peripeteia*, is Crito's revelation that Glycerium is Chremes' daughter; the solution, or dénouement, is the satisfaction both of Pamphilus and of Simo by a marriage with Glycerium. That is, Philumena (strictly in herself) is of no importance: she exists merely to help provide the "question." On the other side, if we raise our eyes from mere charts or machinery, we may ask what becomes of Philumena when Pamphilus "deserts" her: we should like to "see her settled." Hence the insertion of Charinus to make ready for this; hence, too, the spurious variant of the final scene, which dilates upon Philumena's marriage. The most exact statement is that Charinus has an excuse for his presence, but he is a bungle because he does not help the real plot.

That is to say, in the *Andria* we are present at the birth of a notable dramatic expedient. In all his plays Terence bifurcates the plot — thinks it out and works it out in two parts that are necessary to each other. This device must by no means be confused with the underplots familiar in Elizabethan drama. It is not merely that the two parts of a Terentian comedy together form the whole as two gloves make a pair: they are complementary, as is one blade of a pair of scissors to its companion. This duality-method is the centre, the focus, of Terentian art and the Terentian spirit: both his vivid moral sense and his magnificent dramatic talent lead him to this principle of duality in unity. So far as can be learned, it is entirely his own — another, and the most impressive, proof of his originality not merely in play-conception but in play-construction also. For he actually recasts his " original " in order to secure this dualism. He tells us this concerning the *Heautontimorumenos* in so many words, though few care to listen. So in the *Andria:* that duality-method which is good in *Self-Punishment,* excellent in *Phormio,* magnificent in *The Brothers,* is here crudely thrust upon us. It works badly, but its very badness makes it unmistakable. The improvement to which so many allusions have been made is clearest of all in this basic element of Terentian art.

*Self-Punishment,* the author tells us in his prologue (v. 6), is a " two-fold play made out of a single plot " — *duplex quae ex argumento facta est simplici.* That he should so handle a " single " or " simple " Menandrian comedy as to secure the duality-structure shows how vital it was in his eyes. His skill here shows a decided advance on the *Andria.* The two groups — Clinia, his father Menedemus, and his mistress Antiphila; Clitipho, his father Chremes, and his mistress Bacchis — are of tolerably equal importance. The love-troubles of Clinia and of Clitipho settle one another by an admirable interlocking that far transcends the mere juxtaposition of the preceding drama.

Menedemus, before the action opens, is so enraged by Clinia's keeping a mistress that by his reproaches he has caused his son to go off to the wars. But he misses Clinia, and soon deeply repents his own harshness: in order to punish himself, he toils early and late with spade and ploughshare, old though he is. Thus, when Clinia returns, Menedemus is eager to indulge him; but his old neighbour Chremes, fearing that this new extreme may spoil Clinia, induces him to pretend that he is still harsh and to allow himself, as if unconsciously, to be swindled out of the money that Clinia needs. This odd arrangement helps Clitipho, whose mistress Bacchis, being vastly more expensive than Antiphila, is in pretence substituted for her with disconcerting but laughable results. Nevertheless, the duality-scheme is not perfect. Not only should it secure Clinia's permanent happiness with Antiphila — she proves, as a matter of fact, to be Chremes' daughter and marries Clinia: it should also put the Clitipho-Bacchis affair on a " satisfactory " footing. This does not happen: Bacchis vanishes after the Third Act, and Clitipho agrees to marry a lady not hitherto mentioned. This lapse in technique is due to the irremediably undesirable character of Bacchis.

The mining and countermining is marvellously deft but not flawless. Clinia and his slave Syrus know nothing (apparently) about Menedemus' complete change of mind as to

Clinia's extravagance; yet they coolly transfer
Bacchis and her retinue to his house. Also,
there are one or two blind alleys in the discussions concerning all these machinations.
But the chief defect is the complexity itself.
Terence has been too clever. Perhaps no one
is able, perhaps no one except Terence himself ever has been able, to give from memory
a complete and accurate account of this plot:
far more to the purpose, it may be doubted
whether any Roman auditor could follow it.
Menedemus is to know that he is not being
fooled as Chremes thinks he is, and is to tell
Chremes, so as to fool him, that he is not
being fooled as he intended to allow himself
to be. The stalwart sons of Romulus must
have found this trying. Even a modern
reader, who can go as slowly as he wishes,
must keep his wits about him. Menander
wrote the play " simple "; it is Terence who
has introduced this eye-defeating complexity.

In the arrangement or development we observe a brilliant novelty. Terence takes the
conventional idea, a slave's device to extract
from the old master funds for his young master's amour. He also adopts the equally
familiar discovery that the heroine is of free

Athenian birth and so may legally marry her lover. But he sets this discovery in the centre of the action, not at the close as usual, thus dislocating the traditional procedure by forcing Syrus to begin his money-plots afresh. Nor has Syrus a moment to lose: he only just prevents Clinia from revealing Clitipho's connexion with Bacchis by departing without her to Menedemus' house, despite the foregoing pretence that Bacchis is his mistress, not Clitipho's.

THE *Eunuch* exhibits a queer yet fascinating jumble of qualities. Consider first our main topic of plot-construction. Repenting (it would seem) the extreme elaboration, the ruthlessly close interweaving, that marks *Self-Punishment*, Terence here aims at a simplicity that shall yet follow his duality-method. Such success was not to be attained till *Phormio*. Here he has improved his notion of structure without, however, carrying it quite adequately into practice. The parts that in *Self-Punishment* interlocked too tightly can here be heard rattling as they hang together.

The two correlative interests are Phaedria's jealous passion for the courtesan Thais and

Chaerea's rape of Pamphila followed by his
desire to marry her. The interweaving consists herein, that Pamphila is a protégée of
Thais and that Chaerea gains his opportunity
by impersonating the eunuch whom Phaedria
presents to Thais. So far, this is an excellent
bifurcation of interest, as easy to follow as
anything (properly to be called a complication) can well be. But Terence has practised
*contaminatio*. What has just been described
corresponds to the *Eunuch* of Menander. Into
this, as he notes in his prologue, he has inserted the soldier and parasite from Menander's *Flatterer*.

These scenes of Thraso and his hanger-on
Gnatho form a considerable part of our
comedy. Most of them are curiously out of
key with the rest of Terence's work: apparently in an evil hour he tried to imitate Plautus. For it seems plain that the one reason
for this element is the wretched battle-scene
where Thraso deploys his followers in front
of Thais' door: that is why we have so often
been told of Thraso's fancy for Pamphila,
which otherwise has no point or result. And
when the battle does arrive, it is a fiasco not
only for the soldier (of course) but for the

[ 152 ]

playwright also. Having set his heart on a scene of boisterous farce, he leads up to the rally with some elaboration and then allows all the fun to slip through his fingers. Plautus would have done it much better; in *Ralph Roister Doister* it is carried through with capital fun and boundless verve.

Why, then, is this written in at all? Thraso restores Pamphila to Thais, but why need they have been separated? Only to give Thraso a *locus standi*. Again, Thais' wish to conciliate him is made her excuse for temporarily dismissing Phaedria; but there is no reason in the main plot for such dismissal. Chaerea's outrage could not have been committed had not Thais left home — to dine with Thraso; but why such elaboration to secure her absence, which could easily have been caused and arranged otherwise in three lines? Evidently Terence sets great store by this element, seeing that he takes such pains to force them into the action. Why? The explanation is found in that disgusting final scene, where Thraso is induced by his longing for Thais' society unconsciously to finance the liaison between her and Phaedria. Terence is insisting on his duality. Chaerea's affair is settled by

[ 153 ]

a discovery that Pamphila is of free Athenian birth. Thais is not, but she has shown herself throughout a wise, resourceful, and charming woman. Therefore Phaedria is to be permanently happy with her, a result secured by a steady and quasi-respectable concubinage. Funds for this can be secured only through Thraso. On moral grounds we may condemn this vigorously; at present we are to observe that Thraso proves necessary to the duality-method. The dualism would have been perfect had Thais been legally possible as a wife for Phaedria.

The main plot is masterly. Thais' dismissal of Phaedria brings out beautifully his jealous passion and the loving patience of his mistress. Chaerea's plan to impersonate the eunuch, and its outcome, are brutal and heartless, but they give excellent dramatic results. His success engenders in him a sincere love: when he learns that Pamphila can marry him he bursts into a rhapsody of delight. Further, the discovery of his offence brings out the sound character of Thais as does nothing else. Throughout the comedy she shows herself a worthy successor of Chrysis in the *Andria* and foretells the noble Bacchis of the *Hecyra,* but her great moment comes when she rebukes this reckless young scoundrel[98] (864 ff.):

> *nec te dignum, Chaerea,*
> *fecisti: nam si ego digna hac contumelia*
> *sum maxume, at tu indignus qui faceres tamen.*

"Chaerea, you have done what is unworthy of you. Even if I entirely deserve this insult, you should have been above inflicting it." Chremes, again, Pamphila's brother, is used to throw light upon Thais: his drunken vacillation, when the "battle" threatens, is turned to firmness by her encouragement. At the close she gains even the father's affection. Another delightful feature is the passage (968 ff.) where tradition is made to stand on its head. Pythias, seeking revenge on Parmeno, terrifies him by her account of the punishment about to be inflicted upon Chaerea. In panic he reveals everything to his old master on his own initiative — a laughable reversal of the trite system whereby the *senex* threatens flogging and other horrors in order to extract the scandalous truth.

IN *Phormio* Terence's constructive skill reaches perfection. We shall observe in the

two following plays that this skill is applied
with greater resourcefulness and flexibility, as
with deeper feeling and richer wisdom, but he
has now at last gained complete mastery of
his instrument. He has learned the double
lesson of *Self-Punishment* and of the *Eunuch*.
All is beautifully orchestrated, so that even a
spectator could follow every detail with comfort: the various interests of Antipho, Phaedria, Demipho and Chremes, dominated and
driven by Phormio with pervasive activity and
tireless ingenuity, make this comedy a delight,
not a puzzle. The duality-method also is here
at length perfected. Antipho, son of Demipho,
dreads being compelled to give up his beloved
wife Phanium and marry his cousin, daughter
of Demipho's brother Chremes. Phaedria, son
of Chremes, is in love with Pamphila, a slave
owned by Dorio, and is at his wits' end for
money to buy her freedom, for she is about to
to be sold to the usual officer and taken by him
away from Athens. These two difficulties are
made to solve one another by the talent and
impudence of Phormio, one of the most en-
gaging scoundrels in the rich annals of the
stage.

Before the play opens he has brought

[ 156 ]

about Antipho's marriage, while Demipho and Chremes are abroad, by pretending to be Phanium's relative and so bound, under Attic law, either to find her a husband or to marry her himself. He therefore brought a lawsuit against Antipho to compel him as next-of-kin to marry her. Antipho intentionally lost the case and took her though she had no dowry. Demipho on his return is furious at Antipho's apparent supineness. The young husband in terror hides himself and Phaedria defends him to Demipho, who exclaims (267) *tradunt operas mutuas* — "they help each other turn and turn about": the words are a capital description of Terence's method. Demipho and Chremes offer Phormio five *minae* — the legal minimum — to take Phanium back. This he contemptuously refuses; but we shall find that the offer gives him an idea. Next, our attention is transferred to Phaedria and his trouble about Pamphila. He pleads abjectly with Dorio for three days' grace in which to find the thirty *minae* for her purchase, but the slave-dealer is obdurate. Then Antipho intercedes — *tradunt operas mutuas* — and, with Geta, prevails on Dorio to allow them until tomorrow morning. Phormio evolves a scheme to extract the required thirty *minae* from the two fathers. He sends Geta to report to them that Phormio would have been glad to marry Phanium himself, but she has no dowry and he has debts. So he has become engaged to a lady who has a dowry. Now, if Demipho will pay him what he needs (thirty *minae!*), he will break off his engagement and marry Phanium. Demipho is enraged, but Chremes is so eager to see Antipho his daughter's husband that he volunteers to pay, out of the rents of his wife's property which he has just brought home from Lemnos. Phormio receives the money, pays Dorio, and delivers Pamphila to Phaedria, whose difficulty is now overcome.

But what of Antipho? We are told (705 ff.) that Phormio will find some excuse for not taking Phanium from him after all. But is the scheme handsome enough? Surely so lame and precarious a solution would be unworthy of a fine worker like Phormio. The requisite brilliance is made possible by an opportune discovery that he is not the only rascal in the play. Chremes has throughout been nervously intent on a marriage between Antipho and his daughter. But who is she? We learn that she is not the child of his Athenian wife Nausistrata. His voyage to Lemnos had for its object not only the collection of Nausistrata's rents, but also a visit to — his wife and their daughter, who had however left for Athens. Chremes is a bigamist. It is this Lemnian girl whom he wished Antipho to marry, since his brother's son would be less likely to make trouble about his bigamy. When the two fathers go in to arrange for Phanium's dismissal, it is found that Phanium is the very daughter in question. Thus Antipho's marriage is safe, and is now at once used to help Phaedria's amour — *tradunt operas mutuas.*

In a scene of delicious light comedy Demipho and Chremes coolly ask Phormio to return the thirty *minae,* since Phanium is not leaving Antipho after all. Phormio protests against this shilly-shallying and calls on them to send him his "wife." Demipho scoffs bitterly, but Phormio blandly goes on to explain that he has another woman's cause to defend. Amid the agitated groans of Chremes he airily discourses of Lemnos and bigamy: he will reveal all to this wronged lady Nausistrata. Chremes is for leaving him in possession of the money, but Demipho urges him to desperate

courage and they fall upon their too-virtuous
opponent.[99] He cries aloud for Nausistrata,
who comes out and learns everything. Chremes
is utterly humiliated and Phaedria is allowed
to keep Pamphila — Chremes' own wife asks
him (1040 f.): "Do you think it a scandal for
a young man to have one mistress when you
have two wives?"

THE *Mother-in-Law* is unique among Terentian plays in one particular at least: indeed it
would probably be hard to find many parallels
in the whole of dramatic literature. That peculiarity is the splendid boldness and success
wherewith it accepts traditional theatrical data
and proceeds charmingly and skilfully to stand
tradition on its head. That is why it failed in
Rome and is despised or ignored by modern
critics. Mr. Shaw did the same thing when
he wrote *Arms and the Man*. What could his
innocent audiences make of a play that, start-
ing well with the resplendent military hero (in
the cavalry, of course), the idolatrous fiancée
awaiting his glorious return, the amusing parents, and the commonplace soldier of the defeated side, suddenly went off the rails and
destroyed itself, depicting hero and heroine

as shams, the unromantic people as genuinely mature and effective human beings? But Mr. Shaw luckily survived, and continued his work. Today most of us understand what he was driving at thirty-seven years ago. The *Hecyra* provides a close analogy with the Shavian play, but unluckily Terence died young. At its first appearances the audience did not hear it to the end owing (among other causes) to the vociferous protests of the ladies in the audience, who, no doubt, were scandalized by the charm and strength attributed to a courtesan. Only at the third attempt was it performed in full, shortly before its author left Rome for ever, as it proved. He could not, like Mr. Shaw, impose himself gradually upon the public by many years of sparkling trenchant original work that pursued this method of constructive disillusionment.

In brief, this is a most beautiful play, composed with such perfect mastery that it is probably unequalled in its own kind; but certain unconventional qualities have prevented many readers from appreciating its peculiar charm. These unconventional features shall be considered first.

First, this is no comedy at all as comedy is

understood by enthusiasts for Plautus, by those who " go to the theatre to enjoy themselves " (meaning either a surfeit of guffaws or a drench of sentimentality), by those who understand by comedies about the relations of the sexes either the airily fanciful like *The Admirable Crichton* or the pornographic like *Le Vieux Marcheur*. Such theatre-goers have often much right on their side. But there are more sorts of comedy than one, or two. The *Hecyra*, judged by the standards both of the Globe Theatre and of the Palais Royal, is certainly an execrable play. But Terence is not attempting to write like Shakespeare or like Rip; this should be absurdly obvious, but it seems to need saying. Our play is pathetic high comedy, not unlike the *comédie larmoyante* evolved by La Chaussée, though it enormously surpasses any work of that forcible-feeble rhetorician. As a result, though the dialogue is aglow with wit in the sense of brilliant aptness, jokes are very rare. Perhaps Pamphilus' hurried description (440 f.) of his imaginary acquaintance is the only example:

*magnus, rubicundus, crispus, crassus, caesius,*
  *cadaverosa facie.*

"Tall, ruddy, curly-haired, burly, gray-eyed — he looks like a corpse."

Next, although traditional characters tread the stage, they act (as we have already said) in defiance of tradition. Terence openly rejoices in this break with stereotyped puppets, machine-made situations: more than once he actually remarks that he is flouting theatrical convention. At the close Pamphilus says (866): "Don't let us manage this affair as they do in the comedies" — *placet non fieri hoc item ut in comoediis.* Indeed, whoever else does not enjoy this play, Terence did. Probably his " slim feasting smile " was least slim while he dealt with Parmeno. That luckless henchman knows well enough what the audience expects of a " knavish valet "; but every time he tramps dutifully onto the stage, his pockets crammed with amulets, his brain agog with cunning devices, his mouth full of *hem, quid ais, heus,* he is ordered off again to make room for the play. This happens repeatedly: the centurions and their wives knew no more what to make of it than their descendants appreciated Saranoff's cavalry-charge, but its preliminary recital must have caused a glorious hour round Scipio's dinner-table. Laches, again, is a very poor specimen of the comic heavy father. He does indeed insult his wife now and then, bringing back a moment's cheer to the bewildered auditor; but on the whole we perceive with growing alarm and resentment that he is a much better man than his son, the "hero," and shows real common-sense, a reasonable grip of the situation. No doubt he loses all sense of theatrical decency because from beginning to end no one makes any attempt to swindle him — enough to unnerve any comic father.

But the least conventional of all is Bacchis. Her defection is not in the least laughable, for Terence is expending all his delicate yet powerful art on the creation of a beautiful character. But here, no less than in Parmeno, he is perfectly aware how he is treating tradition. In the first words of the play he puts forward Syra to lecture young Philotis on the correct practice of a courtesan — the "vampire" method so incessantly depicted today and even then familiar. Bacchis proceeds to do exactly the opposite: some might even say that Terence has over-emphasized her revolt from rule. She is more than willing to help bring Pamphi-

lus' wife back to him, and cheerfully tramples
on professional rules in doing so (774 ff.):

> *Pamphilo me facere ut redeat uxor*
> *oportet: quod si perficio, non paenitet me famae,*
> *solam fecisse id quod aliae meretrices facere*
> *fugitant.*

"It is my duty to see that Pamphilus' wife returns to him. If I do this, I shall not be sorry
to have the repute of doing what all other
courtesans shrink from." Before this climax,
her self-control, discretion and kindness have
induced him to learn, and love his wife; and
now her courage in facing Philumena brings
about the discovery that entirely closes the
breach between husband and wife and between
their parents. She is a splendid and delightful
woman, the fulfilment of Chrysis and Thais.
Her interview with Laches makes a superb
scene. He expects a woman of Syra's school,
to be overawed and bribed: he finds a vibrant
spirited personality (734 f.):

> *ego pol quoque etiam timida sum, quom venit in*
> *mentem quae sim,*
> *ne nomen mihi quaesti obsiet; nam mores facile*
> *tutor.*

"Indeed, I am nervous too, when I consider what I am — lest the name of my trade should injure me: for my conduct I can defend easily." Before this wonderful scene closes, a great figure has been added to the world's drama.

The third and last peculiarity of the *Hecyra* concerns plot-structure. In outline the story runs thus. Pamphilus, despite his passion for Bacchis, was induced by his father Laches to marry Philumena, daughter of Phidippus; but he has been her husband only in name. He seeks Bacchis, but she has ignored him; this, and Philumena's sweet patience, have turned his heart to his wife. But he has to go to Imbros on business, leaving his wife with his parents, Laches and Sostrata. Later, Philumena left them for Phidippus and Myrrina, and refused to return, alleging illness. Laches thinks his wife to blame for this estrangement. Pamphilus comes home, definitely in love with Philumena: he is convinced that he must choose between her and Sostrata. He hears that Philumena is ill, rushes in, and finds that she has been delivered of a child, which he knows cannot be his. Myrrina appeals to him. Her daughter (she explains) was outraged

by some man unknown, before her marriage:
that is why she left Laches' house; Pamphilus
alone "knows" that he himself is not the
father: let him keep the secret; the child shall
be exposed. To this Pamphilus agrees, but he
is determined not to take his wife back; this
refusal puzzles Laches and Phidippus. Soon
Phidippus discovers his grandchild and in-
forms Laches. Pamphilus refuses to take
Philumena back even despite the birth of the
child, and makes the supposed quarrel between
Sostrata and Philumena his excuse. Sostrata
and Laches offer to withdraw from Athens, but
even this does not alter his intent. The fathers
in angry amazement conclude that this obsti-
nacy can be due only to the continued ascend-
ancy of Bacchis. Laches sends for her and
insists that she give his son up. Bacchis tells
him the facts, which he asks her to convey to
the ladies. She goes within for this purpose,
and discovers by means of a ring that Philumena's unknown assailant was Pamphilus himself. All ends happily.

But no such bald summary can do justice
to the flawless mastery of construction here,
the gracious charming flexibility whereby character moulds plot and plot reveals character.

[ 167 ]

Consider the different reasons that cause Bacchis to confront Philumena: you will find character after character slowly giving up their
essence under your contemplation. Perhaps
the most beautiful device is that the same
event, the child's birth, makes Laches still
more eager to receive Philumena back and
Pamphilus still more resolute not to agree —
both for excellent reasons. So might one con-
tinue to enjoy now the quiet beauty, now the
thrilling deftness, again the lingering fra-
grance, of this matchless drama.

The peculiarity whereof we spoke at first
concerns the duality-method. What becomes
of it here, in one of the two finest works that
Terence has left? It seems to vanish, for we
find but one pair of lovers. Evanthius points
out this discrepancy in his essay *On Tragedy
and Comedy*.[100] "This further quality in Terence seems to merit praise, that he has chosen
for treatment richer subject-matter, drawn
from double interests (*ex duplicibus negotiis*).
For, except the *Hecyra,* which has only the
love-affairs of Pamphilus, the other five have
two young men apiece." But a little considera-
tion will show the duality-method at work here,
and most dextrously. The uniqueness lies in

[ 168 ]

the interweaving. Whereas the other comedies exhibit two pairs of lovers and two love-difficulties entangled, here the two difficulties exist indeed but concern the same man and woman. The problems are Pamphilus' estrangement from his wife and Philumena's plight owing to the offence of an unknown man. Then these two affairs beautifully merge by the identification of Pamphilus with the offender. The plot-complication is no less consummate than the character-drawing.

*The Brothers* exhibits Terence's most highly elaborated use of the duality-method, in a manner entirely different from the novelty of the *Hecyra*. Here we find two pairs of interests, not one pair as in all the five preceding works.

First, as in *Phormio,* the two love-affairs, of Aeschinus and Pamphila, of Ctesipho and " Bacchis," [101] are employed to solve one another. Aeschinus, on behalf of his timid brother Ctesipho, abducts Bacchis from the slave-dealer: this, becoming known, causes Pamphila's mother to believe that he is deserting Pamphila for Bacchis, and her resistance brings Aeschinus' liaison to the ears of his " father " Micio, who therefore arranges

the marriage of Aeschinus and Pamphila when
their situation was otherwise hopeless. Thus
Ctesipho's affair produces the solution of
the Aeschinus-Pamphila predicament. On the
other side, Ctesipho's difficulty is solved by
his brother's trouble. For his father, Demea,
is induced to acquiesce in his liaison by Aeschinus' appeal, and this appeal has weight exactly because Demea has already decided to
beat Micio at his own game of indulging youth-
ful folly; this indulgence, finally, has been
shown above all, and to Demea's continued
annoyance, in favouring Aeschinus' affair with
Pamphila.

Secondly, Demea and Micio form a separate
couple with conflicting interests. One of
Demea's sons, Aeschinus, has been adopted by
his bachelor uncle Micio and educated in Athens on a system of indulgence and mutual confidence. The other, Ctesipho, has stayed with
Demea and has been brought up in the country
on a system of severity and repression. Each
of the " fathers " believes firmly in his own
method and criticizes his brother's: the kernel
of the play is the clash between these systems.
Here is duality again, applied to a quite different theme from the love-escapades of the

five earlier comedies, another couple of which
is found here also, but as the outcome of
these more fundamental educational doctrines.
Demea and Micio are admirably contrasted.
The latter has been already described. Demea
is not less good, though less novel. He is the
traditional *senex* of a thousand comedies, with
the addition of will-power and sagacity. His
outcries against the corruption of Aeschinus
and the system that has induced it are justified and effective. At the close he dominates
the stage in scenes richly comic, rather touching, altogether wise and instructive.

The value and attractiveness of this climax
are caused by the duality-method once more,
but applied to new material. Micio's failure
and Demea's failure are both repaired by the
lessons that each can read the other. Both
the competing systems are mistaken. A good
number of modern plays have been founded on
the *Adelphoe,* among them Molière's *L'École
des Maris,* Shadwell's *Squire of Alsatia,* Garrick's *Guardian,* Fielding's *Fathers,* Cumberland's *Choleric Man,* and Colman's *Jealous
Wife.* In all these one of the rival theorists
confesses that the other has been justified by
results, and in all except Fielding's the victor

is the person who corresponds to Micio; for the theatre has usually sought to please sons rather than fathers. Terence has been wiser than his successors. Here, as indeed throughout his brief career, technique and knowledge of human nature reinforce and irradiate each other. He knows that extreme and theoretical notions of dealing with men and women, especially the young, cannot produce a sound life. Both these youths have been corrupted. Aeschinus after all has concealed his amour from the sympathetic Micio, and lets matters drift until Pamphila's happiness is in danger. He has no backbone: the system has only made him reckless and insolent, as we observe in that disgusting interview between him and the slave-dealer. He is a bumptious, bullying pseudo-fashionable oaf — the worst kind of oaf. Ctesipho is no worse and no better. Secretive and utterly self-indulgent like his brother, he is also a poltroon: the scene (537–553) where he hides behind the door from his father, too timid to show himself, too nervous to carouse at his ease within, and hysterically whispering to the contemptuous slave who stands between him and detection, is a complete exposure of his depravity.

We return to the climax. A solution of all these troubles, a sound relationship between father and son, is wisely allotted by the playwright to Demea, not Micio, partly through a sense of dramatic balance, Demea having suffered so acutely, partly because he has always realized more deeply the need for a permanently sound way of life for the two youths. First, since Micio has continuously " scored off " him, he determines to beat Micio at his own game, not for the mere fun of the thing but to demonstrate that anyone can grow popular if with an air of *bonhomie* he lets other people have exactly what they want. (Here he is — very naturally — not altogether just to Micio.) This demonstration makes a rather wonderful scene or two, for it is richly farcical and yet all its details proceed from a moral theory and a moral purpose.

He begins with extreme affability to the slaves; next, when Aeschinus complains of the tedious preparations for the wedding, Demea with a wave of the hand exclaims (906): " Let it all go: knock down the back-wall between the gardens and bring your bride through to our house at once, mother, servants and all." These unusual rites come to Micio's ears, as

well they may, and he hurries out to expostu-
late with Demea, who is quite ready for him.
" We ought to help this family," he explains.
" Why, of course," replies his unconscious vic-
tim. " Very well," rejoins the benevolent
Demea. " The bride's mother has no one left
to look after her. *You* should marry her."
Micio splutters in helpless indignation; Aeschinus joins his voice to Demea's; and Micio, now
for years accustomed to give way to his " son,"
surrenders. This is an admirable [102] comic rendering of a serious moral thesis, an appropriate application of his own methods. Moreover, it not only secures the excellent Sostrata's
future: it withdraws Micio from that irre-
sponsible detachment that renders so many
elderly bachelors a public danger. Meanwhile,
Demea sweeps triumphantly onwards: this
poor kinsman Hegio . . . " let *us* give him
that little farm of *yours* . . . don't you remember what you told me yourself: that in
old age we are too fond of money? We must
avoid that fault." Demea is congratulating
himself on hoisting his brother with his own
petard — *suo sibi gladio hunc iugulo* (958) —
when Syrus bustles in to announce that the
back-wall is down. Demea's eye gleams.

Why should the "contriving valet" go un-
recompensed? Has he not crowned his faithful services by helping to abduct Bacchis?
*Non mediocris hominis haec sunt officia* (966)
— "only a remarkable man could have shown
such diligent loyalty": Syrus receives not
only his freedom but that of his wife also
and a "loan" into the bargain. All this settled, Micio in a stupor asks his brother
(984 f.): "What on earth has changed your
character all of a sudden?" Demea answers
gravely and trenchantly, then turns to Aeschinus with a solution of the whole rivalry between the two systems. Both are wrong: we
need a compromise between them. This conclusion is obvious to us modern people, who
advise, and mostly seek to attain, a blend of
elderly wisdom and enlightened sympathy for
the young. But it was less obvious to ancient
Europe. Micio's system was the vogue in the
Athens of Menander, Demea's in the Rome of
Terence. This compromise is a real contribution to practical morality.

Thus the duality-method reaches its height
in this final work of the Terentian genius: the
result arises from neither one doctrine nor the
other, but only from their interaction. And,

as we saw, the same technique is applied to the love-affairs. Moreover, the two sets of duality — if an ugly phrase will be forgiven — are perfectly interwoven, since of course the love-affairs demonstrate the failure of the two competing theories if they do compete instead of blending. It is this exquisitely close yet perfectly intelligible structure, and, within it, the admirable balancing of all the four men, that makes *The Brothers* a perfect masterpiece of high comedy.

# IX. THE BASIC THOUGHT OF TERENCE

LAST of all, something ought to be said concerning topics, themes, or even the "message" of Terence; for here we come upon a chief reason for the frequent opinion that, for all his eloquence, Terence is somewhat pallid, diluted, monotonous. The truth is, he has no topics at all in the usual sense: it would be impossible to prepare any dissertation upon "Politics in Terence" or "The Attitude of Terence towards Sculpture and Painting." The charge of pallor and the rest is in some degree true, as it is true of many others who keep closely to the business of intellectual social comedy. This high urbanity, this slightly fastidious elegance, this chastity of outline in thought and phrase, would consort ill with eloquent outbreaks on politics or atheism, sudden perils or exploits, and frolics, jesting, or horseplay. But, even so, why should not Terence have varied the vivacity, the gusto, of one comedy as compared

with another? This, to be exact, he has done
in the Thraso-scenes of *The Eunuch* and in the
flippancy of Micio. But the first are not successful, and the second is a minor element in
*The Brothers.* In this respect Terence assuredly falls below Menander. Even though
we possess no complete play of Menander, we
cannot mistake the difference in tone between
*Arbitration* and *The Girl of Samos.* Whether
Terence, had he been granted, like his predecessor, another twenty-five years of life, would
have developed in this regard, is a natural but
useless inquiry. We may indeed observe that
his last scene is not merely delightful but novel
— a profoundly important theory of conduct
expounded by means of light fun. Such a description might be applied without too offen-
sive pedantry to some portions of *Henry the
Fourth:* who knows what Terence might have
achieved at fifty? But we shall of course
guard against denying any weakness in him
on the strength of a plea that he might later
have outgrown it. He remains, on this side
of dramatic excellence, a junior Menander.

Let us return to our discussion of topics, or
lack of them. We said that Terence has none
in the usual sense, nothing like Plautus' fre-

quent allusions to public institutions, law, and commerce. Still we can extract — nay, we cannot fail to observe — an important idea concerning human nature itself. And, so far is he from merely obtruding themes or instruction, that his one theory about life has created his dramatic method. His plays are not simply the vehicle of this idea: they *are* the idea, expressed not only by dialogue and action but also by the very shape of his work. This governing idea of Terence is the mutual dependence of human beings. Again and again he causes his people to exclaim that we are sure to err if we walk by ourselves, that others see more wisely in our affairs than we can, that the true life is a life of mutual helpfulness. In his plays the villain is not a slave-dealer or a harsh father or a rapacious courtesan. To heap all the blame for an awkward or agonizing predicament upon the broad shoulders of some artificial bogey ablaze with theatrical fiendishness is easy drama — too easy — but disastrously bad ethics. The real " villain " for Terence is the short-sighted pride that the best of us shows when he seeks to walk alone: the true life is found, not by the excogitation of ethical standards but by human

sympathy. That is why *homo* and its cognates
are so frequent in his writing. His most
famous sentence is also his most emphatic assertion that our great need is not virtue, not
wisdom, so much as a sense of humanity —
*homo sum: humani nil a me alienum puto:*
" nothing human do I count alien to me, for
I too am human." Nothing alien, nothing
" no business of mine " — this feeling explains
Hegio's sturdy championship of his kins-
woman, the self-sacrifice of Bacchis, Chremes'
expostulation with his neighbour's remorseless
toil. Sympathy is the basis of Terentian mor-
als. That is why Terence as a playwright invented and developed the duality-method
whereof we have said so much: his plots con-
sist of two problems that solve each other,
just as in life one man needs and helps his
neighbour. It is the central excellence of Terence that in his work truth and the expression
of truth become one and the same.

# APPENDIX

ADEQUATE discussion of the influence exercised upon English literature by these two poets cannot here be attempted. Three points only shall be made. Firstly, during the Tudor and Stuart periods Latin plays composed more or less after the ancient models were performed on state occasions at the Universities. Of these the most notable are George Ruggle's *Ignoramus,* which delighted James I at Cambridge in 1615, and *Naufragium Joculare* (" The Comic Shipwreck ") by Abraham Cowley, performed at Cambridge in 1638. Secondly, many English plays that cannot be shown to borrow their details from Plautus or Terence have nevertheless been clearly influenced by them: for instance, Congreve's *Double-Dealer* (1693), which is Terentian in its plot-technique and takes its motto from the *Heautontimorumenos.* Thirdly, a good number of plays derive their plot, or parts thereof, from the Latin works either directly or at second-hand. A list of these follows.

### ADELPHOE

*The Scornful Lady.* Beaumont and Fletcher. Before 1609. The similarity is not strong, but there

[ 181 ]

are two contrasted brothers. Morecraft's change of heart (V. i.) reads for a few lines like Demea's, but no motive is assigned for it.

*The Squire of Alsatia.* Thomas Shadwell. 1688. Two brothers contrasted.

*The Tender Husband.* Richard Steele. 1705. The too rigorous discipline of the son is contrasted with the too casual discipline of the wife: see especially the last lines.

*The Jealous Wife.* George Colman the elder. 1761. Based partly on Terence, partly on Fielding's *Tom Jones.*

*The Choleric Man.* Richard Cumberland. 1774. The dedication denies the charge of plagiarism from Shadwell, but acknowledges the debt to Terence.

*The Fathers.* Fielding. 1778. A good deal about competing systems of discipline. Boncour (= Micio) triumphs and Valence (= Demea) is utterly undone. But Boncour accepts his brother's advice and by greater firmness brings his wife to order.

## AMPHITRUO

*Jacke Juggler.* Anonymous. Licensed 1563. Similarity lies in the scene where J. J. pretends to be Careaway, beats him and robs him of his personality. The prologue says that the author has "taken Plautus' first comedy." Notably Plautine style.

## APPENDIX

*The Birthe of Hercules.* Anonymous. Date unknown. Closely modelled throughout on Plautus. Excellent scene of pelting Amphitryon from roof. Amphitryon's anguish when face to face with Jupiter very effective.

*The Comedy of Errors.* Shakespeare. 1589? See under *Menaechmi.*

*The Silver Age.* Thomas Heywood. Printed 1613. The relevant portion is closely modelled on Plautus, but Ganymede replaces Mercury.

*Albumazar.* John Tomkis or Tomkins. 1614. A close imitation of *L'Astrologo* by Giambattista della Porta, printed at Venice in 1606. The only likeness to Plautus lies in the favourite Sosia-beating.

*Amphitryon.* Dryden. 1690. Close imitation, but love-passages between Phaedra and Mercury-Sosia are added; also the venal judge Gripus.

*Amphitryon.* "Altered from Dryden by Dr. John Hawkesworth." 1756. The preface explains that the changes are demanded by Dryden's indecency. Three slips in the plot-work have been removed.

*I and My Double.* John Oxenford. 1835. A farce based on Dryden.

### ANDRIA

*Buggbears.* John Jeffery? 1564 or 1565. Based mostly on Grazzini's *La Spiritata* (pub. 1561) and

Terence. For the Italian element see under *Mostellaria*. There are slight resemblances also to *Adelphoe, Aulularia,* and *Hecyra*.

*The Conscious Lovers.* Steele. 1722. Fairly close following of Terence, with three interesting differences. (i) Charles Myrtle (= Charinus) is so incensed against young Bevil ( = Pamphilus) that he challenges him. Bevil vigorously and successfully voices the author's own objections to duelling. Steele in his preface says that this scene was his reason for writing the play. (ii) Sir John Bevil (= Simo) at the opening asks Old Humphrey (= Sosia) to aid him. Humphrey not only agrees, but (unlike Sosia) does help. (iii) Steele has added some characters and the delightful love-passages between two servants.

*The Perjured Devotee.* Daniel Bellamy. 1739. The preface states that the play was written some years before *The Conscious Lovers*. A considerable part of it is an imitation of Cowley's *Naufragium Joculare;* the rest closely follows the *Andria*. Silvia (= Glycerium) lived formerly in a " monastery ": hence the title. She is secretly married to Valentine (= Pamphilus). Worthy (= Charinus) does not quarrel with Valentine: hence there is no Byrria. Olivia (= Philumena) takes a considerable part. Bellamy explains the action better than Terence, in the pretence of Sir Toby Testy (= Simo) that the wedding is after all to take place,

[ 184 ]

and in the scene of Davus, Mysis, the baby and Chremes.

*The Foundling.* Edward Moore. 1748. Likeness slight. Fidelia was a foundling, sold by a wicked nurse to Villiant, whose evil attempt was baffled by Belmont. The latter, after rescuing her, tries to seduce instead of marrying her, because she has no dowry. But she is found to be a daughter of Belmont's father's friend, and the marriage takes place.

## AULULARIA

*The Case is Altered.* Jonson. Before 1600. Contains two plots, based respectively on the *Captivi* and on the *Aulularia.* Connexion between the two parts is made by Rachel, with whom five men are in love. The *Aulularia* part is excellent. Juniper and Onion are amusing, especially where Onion watches the miser from a tree. The love of Jaques (= Euclio) for his gold is effectively drawn: in V. i. he is lured away from his hoard by a trail of gold pieces laid by the conspirators.

*The Miser.* Thomas Shadwell. 1671. Related to Plautus through imitation of Molière's *L'Avare.*

*The Miser.* Fielding. 1733. The author points out that his work is " taken from Plautus and Molière."

## CAPTIVI

*Supposes* (*i.e.,* " Substitutions "). George Gascoigne. 1566. A close imitation of *I Suppositi*

(1509), by Ariosto, who acknowledges his debt to the *Eunuchus* and the *Captivi*. The latter element is vastly the more important and follows Plautus closely.

*The Case is Altered.* See under *Aulularia*. No reason is given for the interchange of Camillo (= Tyndarus) and Chamont (= Philocrates). Pacue (= Aristophontes) reveals the substitution despite previous threats and for no apparent reason.

### CASINA

*Epicoene; or The Silent Woman.* Jonson. 1610. The only similarity is the masquerade of a man as the bride, which however affects Jonson's plot but slightly.

### CURCULIO

*A Very Woman.* Massinger (and Fletcher?). 1634. Similarity resides only in the scene where the duenna Borachia is made drunk.

### EUNUCHUS

*Ralph Roister Doister.* Nicholas Udall. About 1550. The earliest English comedy. Though it is modelled partly on the *Eunuchus*, partly on the *Miles Gloriosus*, it has no pseudo-classical flavour; a thoroughly delightful play. The *Eunuchus* contributes (i) the assault by the *Miles* (Roister Doister) and his followers, which is immensely better done than in Terence; (ii) the reconciliation at

[ 186 ]

the end by means of the cynical parasite Merygreek
(= Gnatho).

*Supposes.* See under *Captivi.* The part based
on the *Eunuchus* is the escapade of Erostrato, who
pretends to be a servant so as to gain an opportunity of seducing Polynesta.

*The Country Wife.* Wycherley. 1673. Horn-
er's imposture resembles Chaerea's, but his quarry
is miscellaneous.

*Bellamira; or The Mistress.* Sir Charles Sedley.
1687. A close imitation, of small independent interest.

*The Eunuch; or The Darby Captain.* Thomas
Cooke. Printed 1737. Very feeble diluted Terence. No attack on the house. Captain Brag
(= Thraso) was the original kidnapper of
Belinda (= Pamphila). He was also guardian
of Dorinda (= Thais) who naturally wonders
" why my Mother chose him for a Guardian to
me."

## HEAUTONTIMORUMENOS

*Misogonus.* Author uncertain. 1560. As in
Terence Clitipho is brought to his senses by the
discovery that Antiphila is his long-lost sister and
by the decision of their father Chremes, in his
disgust with Clitipho, to settle all his property on
her: so here Misogonus is reformed by the return
of his long-lost brother Eugonus and by the decision

of their father Eugonus to disown Misogonus and make Eugonus his sole heir.

*All Fools.* Chapman. 1599. Follows Terence closely, but adds the affairs of Cornelio and his wife Gazetta. The contriving Rinaldo is himself deluded towards the end.

## MENAECHMI

*The Comedy of Errors.* Shakespeare. 1589? Based closely on Plautus, but adds doubled slaves as in *Amphitruo.*

## MERCATOR

*Albumazar.* See under *Amphitruo.* The father (Pandolpho) is the rival of his son (Eugenio).

*The Citizen.* Arthur Murphy. 1761. A farce ridiculing pretentious and vicious citizens (as contrasted with " men of fashion "). There is rivalry between father and son, which is however worked out quite differently.

## MILES GLORIOSUS

The following plays are extremely dissimilar, but each has a *miles,* whose name is added.

*Thersites.* Anonymous. 1537. Thersites.

*Ralph Roister Doister.* (See under *Eunuchus.*) Roister Doister.

*Endymion.* Lyly. 1585. Sir Tophas.

*Love's Labour's Lost*. Shakespeare. Before 1598. Armado.

*All's Well That Ends Well*. Shakespeare. 1598? Parolles.

*Henry IV, Part I*. Shakespeare. 1598. Falstaff.

*Every Man in His Humour*. Jonson. 1598. Bobadill.

*May-Day*. Chapman. Printed 1600. Quintiliano.

*Henry IV, Part II*. Shakespeare. 1600. Falstaff. Pistol.

*Henry V*. Shakespeare. 1600. Pistol.

*The Merry Wives of Windsor*. Shakespeare. 1602. Pistol.

*A King and No King*. Beaumont and Fletcher. 1611. Bessus.

*The Old Bachelor*. Congreve. 1693. Bluffe.

## MOSTELLARIA

*Buggbears*. See under *Andria*. The element based on *La Spiritata* is the elaborate pretence that the house is haunted by devils. This frightens Amedeus away, much as in Plautus, but the device is used to cover theft of money for a dowry.

*The Alchemist*. Jonson. 1610. The only similarity is in V. i., where Face, by an excuse of the plague and of spirits, prevents Lovewit from entering his own house.

*The English Traveller.* Thomas Heywood. Printed 1633. There are two separate plots, one the touching melodramatic story of the Geraldine family, the other closely modelled on the *Mostellaria*. In the imposture about the purchase of another house, Heywood has not even the dexterity to make Old Geraldine equivalent to Simo, but drags in a new person, Ricot, for the purpose. The *éclaircissement* with Reignald (= Tranio) is much better than in Plautus.

*The Drummer.* Addison. 1716. The " ghost " of Truman plays a drum and terrifies the household.

*The Intriguing Chambermaid.* Fielding. 1733. The contriver is the chambermaid Lettice, who drives away the returning Father (Goodall) exactly as in Plautus. But the play as a whole is based directly on Regnard's *Le Retour Imprévu.*

## PHORMIO

*The Cheats of Scapin.* Otway. 1677. Related to Terence by a close following of Molière's *Les Fourberies de Scapin.*

*Scaramouch a Philosopher.* Edward Ravenscroft. 1677. Fairly close imitation of Terence by way of *Les Fourberies de Scapin,* together with much incredibly flat buffoonery of Harlequin.

*The Man of Business.* George Colman the elder. 1774. A pleasant blend of *Phormio* and

*Trinummus.* The former contributes Golding's
journey to Bengal to fetch his daughter by his
first wife, Mrs. Carlton's greeting him under the
name of Winterton, and the revelation made to
Mrs. Golding by Denier, when cornered, that Lydia
is Golding's daughter. But Mrs. Golding takes this
far more amiably than does Nausistrata.

### PSEUDOLUS

*The English Lawyer.* Edward Ravenscroft. 1678.
Based ultimately on Plautus with feeble additions.
Proximately, it is an adaptation of Ruggle's *Ignoramus* (1614), which is derived from Plautus
through Giambattista della Porta's *La Trappolaria.*

### RUDENS

*The Captives.* Thomas Heywood. Licensed
1624. There are two plots side by side, exactly
as in *The English Traveller.* One is the domestic
melodrama of the Duke of Averne, his wife and
the two friars. The other is a close imitation of
the *Rudens,* though Ashburne (= Demipho) is
very grieved on seeing the shipwreck.

### TRINUMMUS

*The Man of Business.* See under *Phormio.* The
Plautine part is the rescue of Beverley, a young
banker who has gone to pieces in his uncle's absence. Fable saves the situation by apparently

ruining Beverley, for which he is reproached by
Tropick. Tropick, being satisfied by Fable, agrees
to bring money to Beverley (from Fable) as if from
Golding, supposed still in Bengal. He is met and
unmasked by Golding himself. The dedication
says that " Plautus, Terence, and Marmontel, have
contributed to enrich " the play.

# NOTES AND BIBLIOGRAPHY

# NOTES

[The abbreviation B. refers to the Bibliography on pp. 202 ff.]

1. For the distinction between comedy and farce see B. no. 30, p. 1.

2. *E.g. Bacchides,* 1207 ff., *Casina,* 902. The grave moralizing in the first scene of the *Mostellaria* is an inept introduction to what must be taken with a completely light heart if it is to have any chance of success.

3. *Epistles,* II. i. 176; *Ars Poetica,* 270–4. See below, pp. 19 f.

4. X. i. 99. See below, pp. 18 f.

5. See B. no. 34.

6. See below, p. 18.

7. The " old " fragments — that is, those always known to us by quotation in ancient writers — may be most conveniently studied in B. no. 16. During the last forty years many others have been discovered; in particular, extensive and highly important fragments of Menander. These latter will be found in B. nos. 4, 17, 19, and 42.

8. Aelius Donatus " flourished " in Rome, according to his pupil St. Jerome, in 353 A.D. What we now possess has suffered distortion and addition. See B. no. 47, p. XLVI.

9. *E.g.* in B. no 1.

10. See B. no. 20, pp. 464 ff.

11. An allusion to this ends the First Act of *Pseudolus.* Pseudolus says:

> exibo, non ero vobis morae;
> tibicen vos interibi hic delectaverit.

" I shall come back: I shall not keep you waiting. Meanwhile the flute-player will delight you here." Then the Second Act is opened by Pseudolus.

12. Whether the spelling should be Maccus or Maccius

is not certain. The former is given in the prologue of the
*Asinaria: Maccus vortit barbare* — " Maccus has translated
it into Latin." For a full discussion see B. no. 22, pp. 81 ff.

13. Aulus Gellius, III. iii. 14, and Jerome's *Chronicle*,
on the year 200 B.C.

14. Aulus Gellius, III. iii. 3.

15. Cic. *Brutus*, XV. 60: *Plautus P. Claudio L. Por-
cio . . . consulibus mortuus est Catone censore.*

16. Aulus Gellius, I. xxiv. 3.

17. Cp. B. no. 40, pp. 83 f.

18. Aulus Gellius, XV. 24.

19. Quintilian, X. i. 99: *in comoedia maxime claudica-
mus, licet Varro Musas Aelii Stilonis sententia Plautino
dicat sermone locuturas fuisse, si Latine loqui vellent.*

20. In fr. XV of his *Parmeno: in argumentis Caecilius
poscit palman, in ethesin Terentius, in sermonibus Plautus.*

21. *De officiis*, I. xxix. 104: *iocandi genus . . . elegans,
urbanum, ingeniosum, facetum.*

22. *De Oratore*, III. xii. 45: *Equidem cum audio socrum
meam Laeliam . . . sic audio, ut Plautum mihi aut Nae-
vium videar audire.*

23. XXIII. 149: *Graios, Plaute, sales lepore transis.*

24. Cp. note 20 (above).

25. *Epistles*, II. i. 176.

26. *Ars Poetica*, 270–2.

27. See B. no. 23, pp. 134–149.

28. Plautus' debt to Euripides has been discussed, and
probably exaggerated, by Leo. See B. no 22, pp. 113 ff.

29. See B. no. 30, pp. 77 ff.

30. Leo (B. no. 23, pp. 123 f.) connects the Plautine
*cantica* with later Greek lyric poetry.

31. See for instance B. no. 21: " La grande innovation
de Plaute a été d'introduire le chant et parfois la mimique
dansée au milieu d'une action suivie " (p. 11), etc.

32. Livy, VII. ii.

33. *Asinaria*, 11.

34. A. F. West: " On a patriotic passage in the *Miles
Gloriosus* of Plautus," in *The American Journal of Phi-
lology*, VIII. 15 ff. (1887).

35. By Professor E. A. Dale of the University of Toronto.

36. See B. no. 30, p. 60 f.

37. Professor E. A. Dale suggests that the title of the play is derived from this excellent scene. This method of naming comedies was frequent: Menander's *Arbitration* and Plautus' *Rudens* are good instances.

38. The Cook was a very important figure in Middle and New Greek Comedy. See B. no. 30, pp. 42 f., 62 f.

39. See B. no. 21, p. 78.

40. *Elegantia* occurs twice (vv. 19, 23) in *Mercator*, only once elsewhere in Plautus — *Miles*, 1235.

41. Vv. 668 f:

> feci ego ingenium meum,
> reveni, ut illum persequar qui me fugit.

"I have acted according to my nature, and returned to pursue him who avoids me."

42. Other allusions to the audience are found in *Poenulus*, 28, *Pseudolus*, 720 f., *Truculentus*, 931.

43. Euripides, *Hercules Furens*, 922 ff.

44. Euripides, *Hippolytus*, 1173 ff.

45. *E.g.* the lost *Teucer* of Sophocles; cp. Jebb-Pearson, *The Fragments of Sophocles*, II, pp. 214 ff.

46. For a discussion of the vital differences between Plautus' *Amphitruo* and Molière's adaptation thereof, see B. no. 29, pp. 15 ff.

47. Cicero, *de Senectute*, xiv. 50: *quam (gaudebat) Truculento Plautus, quam Pseudolo!* Of *Epidicus* Plautus himself writes (*Bacchides*, 214): *quam ego fabulam aeque ac me ipsum amo.*

48. Especially B. no. 21, *passim*.

49. On Sept. 16th 1850, near Bonchurch in the Isle of Wight. These nineteen admirable lines are printed in his *Miscellaneous Poems*.

50. *Epistles*, II. i. 58: *(dicitur) Plautus ad exemplar Siculi properare Epicharmi.* See B. no. 21, p. 59, 30, p. 109.

51. The fault should probably be laid at the door of the *populus stupidus*, for even Terence finds it necessary to explain the excellent joke with which the *Adelphoe* opens.

52. Cp. *Stichus*, 334 ff. Other "Shakespearean" passages are the disguising of a sturdy youth as Casina ("a great lubberly boy" in the *Merry Wives*), *Pseudolus*, 25 f. ("and whiter than the paper that it writ on Is the fair hand that writ"), and others, of which the most notable surely is *Pseudolus*, 401 ff., the germ of a famous passage in *A Midsummer Night's Dream*:

> poeta, tabulas quom cepit sibi,
> quaerit quod nusquam gentiumst, reperit tamen,
> facit illud veri simile quod mendacium est.

"The poet, when he takes his tablets in hand, seeks for what is nowhere in the world, yet finds it, and makes what is a lie resemble the truth."

53. *Nicomachean Ethics*, IV. 1128a, 22 ff.

54. *Poetics*, XII. 1452 b, 20 ff.

55. This play has two prologues: one in iambics by Euripides, and a beautiful anapaestic passage about Agamemnon's letter, probably written by Euripides the younger for the production of the play after his father's death.

56. The whole passage is entirely non-comic. As Plautus remarks, this play is a tragi-comedy.

57. The most elaborate example of such a scene is *Curculio*, 281 ff. See B. no. 29, pp. 113 f.

58. B. no. 41, p. 188.

59. See B. no. 23, pp. 130 f.

60. B. no. 18 col. 1277; no. 15, p. 90.

61. B. no. 30, pp. 223n., 264, 275 f., 299 f.

62. For other instances see *Casina*, 1006, *Mercator*, 160, 1007, *Persa*, 159, *Poenulus*, 597, 1240.

63. A passage in a recent work on Euripides makes it apparently needful to say that the objection to the *deus ex machina* is not the use of the "machine" as such. Characters who, by the nature of the situation, have to fly (such as Trygaeus on his beetle in the *Wasps*, Iris and Madness in the *Hercules Furens*) are of course carried by the machine. The objection lies against characters introduced at the close to cut the knot, to solve the difficulty of the play arbitrarily.

NOTES

64. Our information about the life of Terence is contained in a short biography written by Suetonius and prefixed by Donatus to his own commentary.

65. The following details come from the *didascaliae* and the prologues.

66. Donatus remarks that Terence has made a mistake: Apollodorus wrote an *Epidicazomene* and an *Epidicazomenos*, the former, not the latter, being the play followed by Terence.

67. These facts are given in the prologue, delivered by the actor Ambivius Turpio.

68. See B. no. 40, p. 118.

69. Cp. p. 18.

70. The passage, from Cicero's *Limon*, is preserved in the *Life* (see above):

tu quoque, qui solus lecto sermone, Terenti,
conversum expressumque Latina voce Menandrum
in medium nobis sedatis motibus effers,
quiddam come loquens atque omnia dulcia dicens.

71. For characterization see note 21. Varro's opinion of his style is reported by Aulus Gellius, VI (VII). xiv. 6.

72. *Epistles*, II, i. 59: (*dicitur*) *vincere Caecilius gravitate, Terentius arte.*

73. X. i. 99: *licet Terenti scripta ad Scipionem Africanum referantur, quae tamen sunt in hoc genere elegantissima et plus adhuc habitura gratiae, si intra versus trimetros stetissent.*

74. The texts for this collaboration are: (i) *Heaut.*, 22–6 (ii) *Adelphoe*, 15–21 (iii) Cicero, *ad Atticum*, VII. iii. 10: *Terentium, cuius fabellae propter elegantiam sermonis putabantur a C. Laelio scribi* (iv) Quintilian (see last note) (v) the life by Suetonius. The latter gives the story (see p. 105) told by Nepos, and the following remark. *Non obscura fama est adiutum Terentium in scriptis a Laelio et Scipione, eamque ipse auxit numquam nisi leviter refutare conatus, ut in prologo Adelphorum,* etc.

75. See the Suetonian *Life*.

76. Vv. 20–27.

77. *Heaut.*, vv. 28–30.

78. *Casina,* 9 ff. This excellent point is made by Leo, B. no. 23, pp. 212 f.

79. See B. no. 48, p. 121; but contrast p. 139: "von der genialen Wildheit des Plautus ganz abzusehen, kann ich nach wiederholter Prüfung mich nicht getrauen, selbst die Übersetzungen des Terenz als Ganzes für Menander zu verwenden."

80. This is badly handled in B. no. 29, p. 11. See B. no. 12, pp. 105 ff.

81. On these words see B. no. 23, p. 246*n.*, no. 12, pp. 98 ff.

82. For instance, Ennius' translation of the opening lines of the *Medea.*

83. See B. no. 38 (August 10), no. 29, p. 141, no. 33, p. 122, no. 13, p. 688.

84. See B. no. 12, pp. 104 f.

85. This assertion (cp. B. no. 29, pp. 6 ff.) has been rejected by Professor Flickinger (B. no. 12, pp. 109 ff.).

86. The topic has been discussed at length in B. no. 29, which received the approval of the late Professor J. S. Phillimore, in *The Classical Review,* XXXIX. pp. 40 f. (1925), but is vigorously opposed in B. nos. 12 and 33.

87. See B. no. 5.

88. Professor Flickinger, *Philol. Quart.,* VI. p. 267 (1927), takes these words "as a frank confession that it is 'a substitute for a new one.'" But this does not suit what follows:

> et is qui scripsit hanc ob eam rem noluit
> iterum referre, ut iterum posset vendere.

89. B. no. 26, p. 50.

90. Another reading is *hoc ibi fit, ubi non vere vivitur.*

91. B. no. 26, p. 88.

92. III. ii: "Though this be madness, yet there is method in 't."

93. *Satires,* II. iii. 259–271.

94. The translation is by Patrick and Prendeville (Dublin, 1829).

95. See pp. 55 f.

96. B. no. 26, p. 22.

97. Davus in *Phormio*, Syra and Philotis in the *Hecyra*.

98. This view of Chaerea is vigorously combated by Professor C. J. Kraemer in *The Classical Journal*, XXIII. pp. 662 ff. (1928). Professor Post (B. no. 33, p. 126) agrees with him.

99. This knockabout scene, though brief, is surprising in Terence. Cp. the fight of the *senes* in Menander's *Samia*. A Terentian play is usually *stataria*, not *motoria* (Evanthius, B. no. 47, p. 22): cp. *Heaut.*, 36.

100. See B. no. 47, p. 20.

101. She is not named in the play, but we may call her so for convenience' sake.

102. Opinions naturally differ about this. See B. no. 29, p. 129*n*.

# BIBLIOGRAPHY

Any attempt to make a small selection from the vast "literature" on Plautus and Terence must be somewhat arbitrary. Still, it is hoped that no vitally important work has been omitted.

1. ALLEN, J. T., *Stage Antiquities of the Greeks and Romans* ("Our Debt to Greece and Rome" Series). New York, 1927.

2. ALLINSON, F. G., Text and Translation of Menander ("Loeb Classical Library"). London and New York, 1921.

3. ASHMORE, S. G., Edition of Terence.[2] New York, 1910.

4. CAPPS, E., *Four Plays of Menander.* Boston, 1910.

5. CLIFFORD, H. R., "Dramatic Technique and the Originality of Terence," in *The Classical Journal,* XXVI. 605–618 (1931).

6. CROISET, M., *Histoire de la littérature grecque,* III, pp. 609 ff. Paris, 1899.

7. DEMIAŃCZUK, J., *Supplementum Comicum.* Krakow, 1912.

8. DUFF, J. W., *A Literary History of Rome from the Origins to the Close of the Golden Age.* London, 1910.

9. ENK, P. J., "De Mercatore Plautina," in *Mnemosyne,* LIII. 57 ff. (1925).

10. FABIA, TH., *Les Prologues de Térence.* Paris, 1888.

11. FLICKINGER, R. C., *The Greek Theater and its Drama.*[3] Chicago, 1926.

12. ——, "On the Originality of Terence," in *Philological Quarterly,* VII. 97–114 (1928).

13. ——, "Terence and Menander," in *The Classical Journal,* XXVI. 676–694 (1931).

14. FRAENKEL, E., *Plautinisches im Plautus*. Berlin, 1922.
15. FRANK, T., *Life and Literature in the Roman Republic*. Berkeley, 1930.
16. KOCK, TH., *Comicorum Atticorum Fragmenta*. Leipzig, 1880–8.
17. KÖRTE, A., *Menandrea*. Leipzig, 1912.
18. KROLL, W., "Komödie (römische)," in Pauly-Wissowa's *Real-Encyclopädie*. Stuttgart, 1921.
19. LEEUWEN, J. VAN, *Menandri Fabularum Reliquiae*. Leyden, 1919.
20. LEGRAND, PH. E., *Daos, Tableau de la Comédie grecque pendant la Période dite Nouvelle* (Annales de l'Université de Lyon). Lyon and Paris, 1910. See also *Loeb*.
21. LEJAY, P., *Plaute*. Paris, 1925.
22. LEO, F., *Plautinische Forschungen.*[2] Berlin, 1912.
23. ——, *Geschichte der römischen Literatur*, I. Berlin, 1913.
24. LINDSAY, W. M., Text of Plautus (Oxford Classical Texts). Oxford, 1903.
25. LOEB, J., *The New Greek Comedy* (abridged translation of Legrand's *Daos*). London and New York, 1917.
26. MEREDITH, G., *An Essay on Comedy*. London, 1919.
27. MOULTON, R. G., *The Ancient Classical Drama*. Oxford, 1898.
28. NIXON, P., Text and Translation of Plautus ("Loeb Classical Library"). London and New York, 1916 etc.
29. NORWOOD, G., *The Art of Terence*. Oxford, 1923.
30. ——, *Greek Comedy*. London, 1931.
31. PERRY, F., *The Comedies of Terence translated into English*. London, 1929.
32. POST, L. A., *Menander, Three Plays*. New York, 1929.
33. ——, "The Art of Terence," in *The Classical Weekly*, XXIII. 121–128 (1930).

[ 203 ]

PLAUTUS AND TERENCE

34. REICH, H., *Der Mimus*. Berlin, 1903.
35. REINHARDSTOETTNER, K. VON, *Plautus. Spätere Bearbeitungen plautinischer Lustspiele*. Leipzig, 1886.
36. RITSCHL, F., *Parerga zu Plautus und Terenz*. 2 vols. Leipzig, 1845.
37. ——, Edition of Plautus. Leipzig, 1884–1890.
38. SAINTE-BEUVE, C.-A., " Térence " in *Nouveaux Lundis* (August 3 and 10, 1863).
39. SARGEAUNT, J., Text and Translation of Terence ("Loeb Classical Library"). 2 vols. London and New York, 1920.
40. SCHANZ, M., *Geschichte der römischen Literatur*. Munich, 1927.
41. SELLAR, A. Y., *The Roman Poets of the Republic*.[3] Oxford, 1889.
42. SUDHAUS, S., *Menandri reliquiae nuper repertae*. Bonn, 1914.
43. TEUFFEL, W. S., *Geschichte der römischen Literatur*. Leipzig, 1910–16.
44. TYRRELL, R. Y., Text of Terence (Oxford Classical Texts). Oxford, 1903. Later (1926) text in same series, ed. Kauer, R., and Lindsay, W. M.
45. USSING, J. L., Edition of Plautus. Copenhagen, 1875–92.
46. WESSNER, P., *Aeli Donati quod fertur commentum Terenti*, etc. Leipzig, 1902.
47. WESTAWAY, K. M., *The Original Element in Plautus*. Cambridge, 1917.
48. WILAMOWITZ-MOELLENDORFF, U. VON, *Menander, Das Schiedsgericht*. Berlin, 1925.

# INDEX

# INDEX

*Daos,* 111.
Davus *(And.),* 141 ff.
Delphasium *(Most.),* 74.
Demaenetus *(Asin.),* 138.
Demea *(Adelph.),* 129 f., 134, 138 ff., 170–6.
Demipho *(Merc.),* 29–53 *passim;* *(Phorm.),* 156–160.
Demophilus, 66 f.
Diabolus *(Asin.),* 75.
Dickens, 55, 82.
*Didascalia,* 16, 29.
Diphilus, 13, 25, 101, 111, 117.
Donatus, 13, 104, 110 ff., 116 f., 123, 129, 146.
Dorio *(Phorm.),* 156 f.
Dorippa *(Merc.),* 33 f., 40 f., 48.
Dossennus, 24.
"Double Law," 39 f.
Dramatic Conventions, 79.
Dryden, 109.
Duality-Method of Terence, 119, 147 f., 151 ff., 168 f., 170 f., 175 f., 180.

Eclogues, 58 f.
*École des Maris, L',* 171.
*Emporos,* 29.
Ennius, 22, 112.
Epicureanism, 45.
*Epidicazomenos,* 101.
*Epidicus,* 16, 20, 27, 53, 57, 72, 96.
Ergasilus *(Capt.),* 83, 86.
Etherege, 36, 133.
Euclio *(Aul.),* 11, 56, 73, 80 f.

*Eunuch,* see *Eunuchus.*
*Eunuchus,* of Menander, 101, 152; of Terence, 10, 101 f., 105, 110, 123 f., 128, 134, 151–5, 156, 178.
Euripides, 22, 68, 72, 76, 112.
Eutychus *(Merc.),* 29–53 *passim.*
Evanthius, 168.
*Every Man in his Humour,* 132.

Faith, 80 f.
Falstaff, 55.
*Fathers, The,* 171.
Fescennines, 23.
Fielding, 171.
*Flatterer,* see *Colax.*
France, Anatole, 104.
*Frau Gittas Sühne,* 109.

Garrick, 171.
Geta *(Phorm.),* 157.
Gillette, Wm., 7.
Giraudoux, 75.
*Girl of Samos, The,* 178.
Glycerium *(And.),* 142, 144.
Gnatho *(Eun.),* 105, 152.
"God from machine," 72, 96.
Goldsmith, Oliver, 133.
Gripus *(Rud.),* 86.
Grumio *(Most.),* 72.
*Guardian, The,* 171.

Hamlet, 13, 36, 128, 131.
Hamlet, 79, 131.
Hanno *(Poen.),* 87.

Trojan War, 45, 75.
*Truculentus,* 21, 53, 63 f., 78, 96.
*Two Gentlemen of Verona, The,* 99.
Tyndarus (*Capt.*), 84, 88 f.

ULYSSES, 75.
Umbria, 15.

VARRO, 16, 18, 103.
*Vidularia,* 16, 21.
*Vieux Marcheur, Le,* 162.
Virgil, 8, 55, 57 f., 120.

*Vis,* comic power, etc., 113 f.
Volcacius Sedigitus, 18, 103.
Volpone, 132.

WASPS, 90.
Way, Dr. A. S. 109.
Weller, 55.
Wilamowitz-Moellendorff, 111.
*Wild Ass,* 66.
Wilde, 133.
Winkle, 82.
Wycherley, 133.

# Our Debt to Greece and Rome

## AUTHORS AND TITLES

# AUTHORS AND TITLES